west marin review

2014

05

A Publishing Collaboration

POINT REYES BOOKS • NEIGHBORS & FRIENDS

VOLUME V • 2014

PROSE

Peter Coyote
Fathers 12

Susan Trott
Plain Jain 25

Judy Brackett
Chicken Crossings 34

Lynn Hoggatt
Madame Alvida Turns a Card 42

Florence Caplow
Elders 58

Frances Lefkowitz
Flash Fiction in Two Parts 64

Tim Foley
Machinery, Waiting 69

Ellen Shehadeh
Shortcake for Breakfast 86

Chris Reding
The Summer Palace Vase 92

Muriel Murch
Morning Rounds 97

Joan Thornton
Maxine 101

Claire Peaslee
The Sand Swimmer 109

Carla Steinberg
Snapshots 117

G. David Miller
Conversations with a Righteous Man 121

POETRY

Gina Cloud
January 7

Laura Juliet Wood
Composting 8

Ryan Connolly
Marsh Hawk 24

Olivia Fisher-Smith
My Wings 32

Howard Norman
Novel Made of Haiku 40

Margaret Stawowy
Vagrant 52

Carolyn Losee
First Miwok Poem 63

Meredith Sabini
Fallen from Grace 82

Judith Shaw
Poem 84

Dean Rader
Notes on Inequality 98

Helen Wickes
Day After Easter 114

Linda Pastan
Peace Process 126

ABOVE Eileen Puppo, *El Patrón*, 1996, ink on paper, 8 × 10 inches

ART + ARTIFACT

Eileen Puppo
El Patrón 2

Bob Kubik
Point Reyes Station 4

Zea Morvitz
Crossed Trunks 7, 80
Inverness Drawing #4 81

T.C. Moore
...in a smooth and flowing manner #5 and *#4* 10, 11

Terry Murphy
Farrier 15

Celt Carr
Self-Reflective Portrait 20

Channon Miles
Self-Reflective Portrait 21

Blaize Adler-Ivanbrook
Self-Reflective Portrait 22

Jennifer Gutierrez
Self-Reflective Portrait 23

Grady Salas Hecht
Invisible World 24

Clare Elsaesser
Flower Child 33

Emmeline Craig
Laundry in the wind with green hills 35

Burt Bacharach, Steven Sater
Living with a Ghost 37

Anna Dal Pino
Investigation of a Raven Investigating Me 47

Kerry Livingston
Blackbirds over the Wetlands 53
Singing by Firelight 65

Claudia Stevens
Traditional Botanical Paintings 54

Britta Kathmeyer
Gossip 61

Sarah Myers
Polka Dot Pathogen 62

Claudia Chapline
New American Garden Book 67

Barbara Vos
Spring Fed 68

Ryan Dunbar
Simple Complexity 75

Carolyn Krieg
Red Deer 79

Timothy W. Graveson
Farm Book 83

Susan Putnam
Untitled #216 85

Randall Gray Fleming
Winter 1 90

Elizabeth Hansen
Green River 96

Debbie Patrick
Are We There Yet? 100

Rebecca Young Winslow
Butterfly Collage 107

Celeste Woo
Nudibranchs 108

Chelsea Buteux
Breach in the Pacific 113
Oncorhynchus kisutch (Coho) 119

Mary Siedman
Arroyo Hondo 116

Wendy Schwartz
Conversation 120

Mark Ropers
Limantour Scoters 127

CONTRIBUTORS 128
GOODS & SERVICES 132
DONORS 139
MASTHEAD 140

Bob Kubik, *Point Reyes Station*, 1995, hand-colored etching, 11¼ × 11¾ inches

Dear Reader

WELCOME TO the *West Marin Review,* now in its fifth incarnation and with a cornucopia of treasures to share. What began as a hopeful idea among neighbors, friends, and a community bookstore in rural West Marin, California in 2006 has evolved into an award-winning journal attracting never-before-published submissions from around the world and from artists in many mediums and writers of all persuasions. Art mediums in this volume range from acrylic to watercolor, with everything in between from knitted nudibranchs to a drawing—or is it a painting?—made of smoke, ink, and pencil. Writers include those with a poetic persuasion, as well as nature writers, song writers, and writers of fantasy, mystery, comedy, and serious nonfiction.

As the reach of the *Review* has expanded geographically, so has the depth of the conversation in its pages about place. This book is not just about geography, urban and rural—it's about our place in the world, within our tribe, inside ourselves. Where do we stand in this wide world? From what perspectives do we see it? These are questions answered not just in prose and poetry, but also by a posse of eighth graders whose teacher arrived on the first day of art class dressed like Frida Kahlo to teach them how to draw "self-reflective portraits" and design and hammer out tin frames.

These are questions also attended to in the several family stories in this volume: Peter Coyote's "Fathers," a vividly physical accounting in stark opposition to Susan Trott's almost-a-drawing-room comedy, "Plain Jain," and David Miller's heady "Conversations with a Righteous Man."

The *West Marin Review* has become known for unexpected diversity that allows first-time writers and artists space alongside contributors many-times published. Poet Ryan Connolly and artist Grady Salas Hecht, both third-graders, share a page across from an author who has published sixteen novels. The unexpected extends in many other directions as well: in Tim Foley's evocative contemplations on San Quentin Prison and the death penalty in California, in Claudia Stevens's botanical paintings from another era, in Randall Gray Fleming's winter scene that will make you want to pull on gloves, and in original music by the iconic American composer, Burt Bacharach, as we rarely see it—a first draft in the composer's own hand. His "Living with a Ghost" is for a new musical, but serves here as a fitting introduction to Lynn Hoggatt's extrasensory "Madame Alvida Turns a Card."

Enjoy the reading—Madame Alvida's and your own. Enjoy a particularly rich collection of arts, crafts, and artifacts in this volume. Some of our closest readers become contributors to future volumes; visit westmarinreview.org for submission guidelines.

POEM Gina Cloud, "January"
ART Zea Morvitz, detail from *Crossed Trunks*, 2011, graphite on Gampi Surface paper, 38 × 25 inches

If the object
is for things to grow
the deadwood must be first to go
then the center
tangled tight
opened wide
to
air and light.

Composting

Laura Juliet Wood

It's a long walk to my compost heap, weeks or months
before I pull on boots,
        stand heavy before the two piles.
                What comes up as I shovel one half

onto the other always surprises me: bottle caps,
purple lace, foil
        from a tenant's barbeque.
                For three years now, plastic soldiers spring

out of nowhere. Whose child? What history, the pieces of
wire and lemon peels
        and dog bones,
                for someone

who doesn't have a dog, knows citrus is slow to decompose.
        The mountain spits up pieces of itself in rock,
                and who's building with these bricks?

I select and set aside nature's more permanent toys:
cactus paddles,
        jacaranda pods and avocado pits,
                the silky husks of bamboo.

They return endlessly as I root through. I am not alone
        on this hilltop: A hummingbird
                in the orange tree, the valley's echo

of drums. We throw it all in, despite advice,
        and it comes back
                black, expectant earth.

T. C. Moore, (opposite) *...in a smooth and flowing manner #5*, 2012, horse hair on canvas, 20 × 20 inches; (above) *...in a smooth and flowing manner #4*, 2012, horsehair and acrylic on canvas, 20 × 20 inches

Fathers

Peter Coyote

MY FATHER, Morris, was only five feet nine inches—a giant to a child—but his nineteen-inch neck and fifty-four-inch chest made him imposing to adults as well, and men marked his presence. He was handsome, with a virile, charismatic manner; a witty man capable of immense charm and extravagant generosity. However, a stratum of magma lay just below his surface, leaking most visibly from his eyes.

Normally animated by a cool, appraising steadiness, those eyes were so dark the irises often appeared as black as his pupils. His gaze communicated a restless, barely sublimated irritation, as if their subject had already claimed more of his attention than it deserved. When he was angry, the intensity of his focus sliced like a paper cut, expressing with unmistakable clarity his intention to dominate or destroy what frustrated his will. He was not incapable of love and sometimes lugubrious Victorian sentimentality. These more tender feelings were not easily expressed to me in a form I could understand.

According to his family, even as a child Morris possessed extraordinary physical strength, which he further developed as a boxer, Greco-Roman wrestler, and black belt in judo. In a sepia-toned snapshot from his college days, he is lifting the front end of a Stutz-Bearcat car off the ground for the amusement of his friends. By seventeen, preternaturally muscled and "cut," in today's jargon, he became a sparring partner of Philadelphia Jack O'Brien, the Boxing Hall of Fame heavyweight most famous for being willing to fight men of any weight and color. Morris worked with Jack on a regular basis, lying about his age, until one day, crossing the Charles River on his way back to the MIT campus, he could not remember whether he was coming from or going to the gym. He abandoned boxing "to save my mind," he said.

His mind was by all accounts worth saving. Besides winning early admission to MIT at age fifteen, he played chess every week with his friend, master player and chess author Edward Lasker, who once played twenty simultaneous games in our house by memory, sitting alone in the living room, while his opponents clustered around the dining room table marking his moves on their boards to keep track. My father loved the rigor and competition of chess strategy and counter-strategy.

Morris made his first money anticipating the Depression and selling short for a boss who made a killing and rewarded him. He had an extraordinary facility with numbers, and that skill served to build up a large investment house and several other businesses, all of which thrived. By the time I was able to follow his conversations, it was apparent he possessed encyclopedic knowledge about a vast array of subjects, claiming that such breadth was required of him to be good at his various activities.

His activities were indeed varied. My father is credited with having "invented" the over-the-counter market in New York, where he owned his own Wall Street investment firm. He became an expert in museum-quality American and English Colonial antique furniture and silver. In addition, he and a partner got into the cattle business, introducing Charolais cattle to the United States by painting black spots on the huge white French animals they had imported into Mexico. They ran them across the Rio Grande as Holsteins to elude the ban on the breed enjoined by the American Angus and Holstein lobbies. Among Morris's other business interests, he was a principal in the Phoenix-Campbell Oil Company and president of the Hudson-Manhattan railroad. He was not Mitt Romney-rich, but he was rich enough to do damn near anything he wanted.

My father's family were immigrants, but they were wealthy, secular, and cosmopolitan. His father, Benjamin "Jack" Cohon, an Uzbek from a family of loggers and tanners, had made an early living as a carnival strongman lifting a horse in a harness attached to a leather cinch at his waist by climbing parallel ladders. When I was a boy he delighted me by folding a handkerchief in his palm and laying the head of a heavy nail against it so that the point protruded between the fingers of his closed fist. Then, with a short, lethal punch he would drive it so deeply into a wooden door that I could not pull it out. He was also a successful inventor and a gifted artist. Years ago, poring over the family papers, I found a patent for a gasoline-operated machine gun he had designed and for which he had been commissioned a captain. He had had his own laboratory at the Corning Glass Works. When, later, he could not make a living as an artist he became a sign painter for the United Cigar Stores and eventually rose to vice president of the company. When he lost all his money in the Depression, he walked into the house, rocked back a shot of Scotch, and left again, taking a job as a cab driver the same day. In his fifties, he founded a lamp factory that endured to support his family.

No child understands how people as immense and powerful as their parents can be compromised and crippled by psychic history. My father was the product of two complex parents. His mother, Rae, was a proud and clannish Sephardic Jew from an ancient line, certain of her superiority over all others and especially the Eastern European Jews known as Ashkenazim—my mother's people. Rae carried herself

Terry Murphy, *Farrier*, 2012, oil on panel, 12 × 16 inches

with the judgmental attitudes and high-status reserve of an aristocrat, and her pitiless gaze was cold as a raptor's.

Beneath an aura of Sephardic physical beauty and Uzbek power, a carmine strain of violence was passed down to my father through both bloodlines. For example, when Jack's horse bit him, my grandfather killed it with a hand sledge, striking it so brutally in the forehead that it collapsed in its own footprint like a demolished highrise. The year after Jack killed the horse, while clearing leaves in his yard, he stepped on the tines of a rake, smashing himself painfully in the face with the handle. For my father, still in short pants, it resembled a comic turn in a vaudeville slapstick routine, and he laughed aloud involuntarily. Maddened by pain, bleeding from his nose, and enraged at being ridiculed, Jack turned vengefully on his six-year-old son.

"You little son of a bitch," he spat, and chased him with such obvious murderous intent that Morris fled into the house, screaming for help. He scrambled up one flight of stairs and then another, terrified and calling for his mother, inches ahead of Jack's grasping hands. Morris turned into the steep, narrow stairway to the attic and slammed the door shut behind him, holding it fast with his feet and wedging his back against the stairs. Alas, he had smashed the door on his father's fingers. Jack screamed with pain and rage while Morris, gibbering with fear, remained paralyzed, afraid to release the door.

In a paroxysm of wrath, Jack stove the door off its hinges with his shoulder and seized his terrified son. When Grandma Rae arrived to investigate the uproar, all of Jack's will was intent on squeezing their son's shoulders through the small circular window in the roof's peak, three stories above the ground. Unable to get through to him with either entreaties or physical strength, Rae finally bludgeoned him with a heavy brass lamp, knocking him unconscious and saving her son's life.

I was the age my father had been at the time, six or seven, when I first heard this story. The night I heard it, Dad, Rae, and Jack were sitting at our kitchen table laughing, sipping neat whiskey, and playing klabiash, a complicated Eastern-European card game. They raised their hands high, slapping down their cards with relish. As they drew and tossed their cards, they recounted this ancient tale with high merriment, while I looked on, confused, uncertain, transfixed. Their faces were flushed as they choked with laughter and my grandmother beamed with satisfaction, proud of her strength and the determination that had vanquished a man of such power.

Struggling with incomprehension and rising horror, I observed them, as vivid as actors on a movie screen. They were physically dense, radiating power and confidence, apparently impregnable, nothing like the restrained parents of my playmates. Fear and doubt seemed foreign to them. They were an alien species roaring with laughter about a father's attempt to murder his son.

Many of my early impressions of my father were either of a force projecting itself through space or of his merriment and love of laughter. He surrendered to laughter, slapping his legs, weeping with joy, and sobbing for breath. It was such an amazing display that it never failed to delight my sister and me.

But Morris was as quixotic and changeable as a tempestuous day, his emotions undependable and uncertain. On a good day he might tousle my hair and laugh at something I did or failed to do. In the next moment he might be distracted, irritable, or angry. Not knowing what to expect galvanized my attention to him. I studied his certainty and his forcefulness as if he were a textbook on manhood, trying to determine how he managed it, how he asserted his will and expected compliance.

The place where I came closest to getting what I sought from him was our farm, called Turkey Ridge. This was the great love of Morris's life, a two-hour drive from Englewood, New Jersey on the border with Pennsylvania, just a few miles south of the Delaware Water Gap. The gap was a deep notch in the Appalachian Mountain range carved out hundreds of millions of years ago by the river and tectonic collisions. Perhaps he loved it so much because the evidence of vast forces that could cleave mountains was clearly visible there.

It was an old homestead and farm on about 150 acres. The solid nineteenth-century house with clapboard sides stood on a stone foundation. Next to the house was a small shed, and next to that was a large, two-story barn. The property had a machine and repair shop that could hold six vehicles, and an old manager's cottage my dad used as an office, also painted barn red and, like every building on the property, topped with local slate from the Bangor quarries.

Morris spent every moment he could there. The farm's thriving cattle business eventually generated more income than his Wall Street firm. He drew the blueprints for additional barns and sheds himself, and he acquired property ceaselessly, until by the time of his death, he owned six farms and nearly three thousand acres of land. From the time I was six, we summered there and spent as many weekends as my mother would bear. When she could bear no more, or when it was too cold, icy, or rainy, Morris went to Turkey Ridge by himself, leaving at the slightest excuse. A patter of rain on the roof in Englewood would move him to call his chauffeur to deliver him to the farm so he could sleep in the rain there. On snowy mornings when I was with him, I often found him in a sleeping bag on the farmhouse porch, huddled against the stacked cordwood and drifted over with snow, sleeping like a baby. I never saw Morris happier anywhere else and especially in inclement weather. Nor did I ever understand how the side of him that relished hunkering down against the elements dovetailed so seamlessly with the part of his personality that demanded comfort and indulgence.

I received Morris's best there as well. As soon as he reached the farm, his mood lightened. The concerns and tensions of Wall Street and making money evaporated. While I was free to wander the woods, hunt for snakes, fish, and daydream to my heart's content, he'd change into his long-sleeved Henley undershirt, his black hat, sheepskin vest, and boots, and dive into the life of the place, working at his blacksmith's forge forcing cherry-red iron to his will, and with his farmhands, planning, repairing, branding, and medicating the animals, deciding which fields would be for hay and which for grazing, assessing the equipment, and deciding about repairs and purchases. This was the concrete life of the body and the solvable problems that he really adored, and I received the spillover of his affections.

During the heavy summer rains, when the sky lowered, the thunder cracked, and the air felt dense enough to wear, he would sometimes gather me under an arm and climb to the top of a haymow in a newer barn, directly beneath the slate roof. Wrapping us in a rough horse-blanket, he sipped pear brandy until he fell asleep and, enveloped by the sound of the drumming rain, I lay beside his enormous chest, which sheltered me like a cliff face. There has never been a rainy day in my life since when these memories have not returned as mnemonics of childhood happiness and safety. He had chosen to be with me, and at such moments my heart would open as only a needy boy's can, and I loved him totally, without measure or reproach.

Self-Reflective Portraits

SPONSORED BY GALLERY ROUTE ONE

Celt Carr, *Self-Reflective Portrait*, 2013, tin, watercolor paper, watercolor pencils, 11¾ × 11¾ inches

---

These portraits are a rite of passage for eighth graders at West Marin School as they are moving into high school. It is a project of the local Gallery Route One's Artists in the Schools program, conceived of and taught by Bolinas artist Vickisa in the style

Channon Miles, *Self-Reflective Portrait*, 2013, tin, watercolor paper, watercolor pencils, 11¾ × 11¾ inches

---

of Frida Kahlo. She asks the artists to look inside themselves for inspiration. What is important to them becomes part of the background for their mirror-images and influences the designs hammered into each individualized frame.

Blaize Adler-Ivanbrook, *Self-Reflective Portrait*, 2013, tin, watercolor paper, watercolor pencils, 11¾ × 11¾ inches

Jennifer Gutierrez, *Self-Reflective Portrait*, 2013, tin, watercolor paper, watercolor pencils, 11¾ × 11¾ inches

Marsh Hawk

Ryan Connolly, Grade 3

I taste mole.
I am in my nest with my mom,
I am a chick.
I eat moles like marshmallows.
I love the marsh,
with no giants
to tread on me.

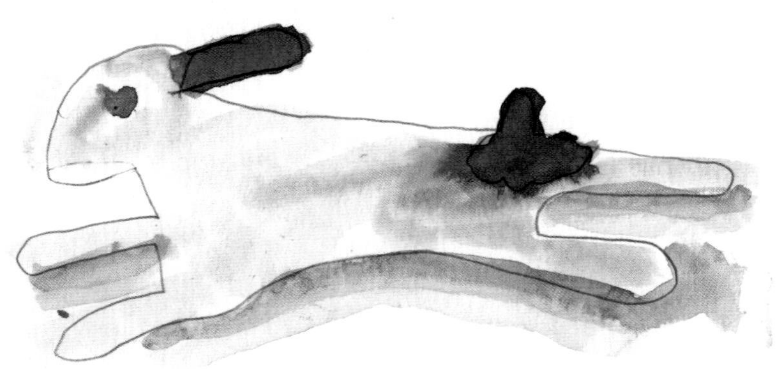

Grady Salas Hecht, Grade 3, Tomales Elementary School, *Invisible World*, 2011, pencil and watercolor, 8½ × 11 inches

Plain Jain

Susan Trott

NELL FOUND the volume about Jainism in her father's library, read it, clasped it to her seventeen-year-old breast, and declared that she had found the answer to the meaning of life and how to live it. So as to cherish it more, she kept it a secret until spring vacation from boarding school, when she shared it with her older brother, Morgan, who was home visiting from California; shared it joyfully, as if telling of her first love affair.

Morgan was ten years older, a half-brother actually, which was lucky for him, Nell thought, because for sure he got their father's brains, not her silly mother's. She admired Morgan immensely because he drank and gambled and wrecked cars (anathema to any Jainist, but never mind) and was so smart he would know what Jain was and not mock her very much about it.

Small, dark, and handsome, he resembled her mother more than their mutual father, only without her mother's trembling hands. "How wonderful," he commended her. "How unique of you, little sister. Where I live the landscape is littered with non-Judeo-Christians such as Zen Buddhists and Sufis, but I have not come across one Jain, unless some of the storekeepers I see sweeping their stoops are Jains. Please don't tell me you are going to carry a broom and sweep the way in front of you so as not to step on insects."

"I am! I thought perhaps a long-handled whisk—a pretty one. Peacock feathers are traditional but a long handle isn't. The handle is important to me because I read about a village someplace where the women all had bowed backs. They thought it was genetic and then someone realized all their brooms had short handles."

"Maybe," said Morgan, "it became genetic Darwinesquely: survival of the bowed-downest. Anyhow, I read this wonderful novel recently wherein the protagonist said she could never become a mystic, as she had too many errands to run. I figure you have five years before you have to run errands."

"I don't intend to be a mystic. I shall be a plain Jain."

Blushing over his laughter, Nell said, "I didn't mean it to sound funny. I'm serious."

"Your mother," said Morgan, "will be very disappointed that you won't make your debut. I believe being a debutante is proscribed in Jainism."

Some days later, having lemonade together, Nell's mother informed Nell's father, "Our daughter has joined a cult. I don't know how it happened that someone absconded with her and brainwashed her while she was ostensibly safe at boarding school."

Emma was small, dark, and beautiful, with haunted eyes. Her husband looked like Robert Redford, only fatter and balding, with a white mustache. In the living room was a portrait of him as a young man looking more like Redford than the movie star, with fewer moles. They sat together in a screened-in porch overlooking a lumpy field decorated with old patches of snow. "Nell used to love horses, now it's Jainism. She says she won't make her debut after she graduates. I suppose she'll be too busy eating brown rice and lentils and wasting away."

Nell's father wondered, as always, why Emma pretended ignorance. Was it to amuse herself, to amuse him, or to position herself to later surprise the unwary listener (him) with her thorough knowledge? Or, on some subjects, such as this one, was she truly the airhead Nell was determined to believe her mother to be?

"Jain is not a cult," he said gruffly, either informing her or playing along, time would tell which. "It is one of the ten great religions."

"Really? What are the other nine? Christian, of course. Judaism. One doesn't say Christianism, does one?"

"No, one doesn't. It is the only one that is an *ity* not an *ism.*"

"Good. Then there's the terrorist religion. Muslim."

There, thought Emerson. There she goes from playful kitten to crouching tiger and smites me by promptly naming, or getting me to name the only religion besides Christianity that isn't an *ism*, proving me misinformed right off the bat.

"Islam. Which, by the way, means peace." I'm not really misinformed, he briefly allowed himself to sulk. I knew it wasn't an *ism.*

"I guess the reason it's not an *ism,*" she said kindly, "is because it contains those three letters already and it would seem redundant to say Islamism. Well, that's four religions. Six to go. But what shall we do about Nell? Morgan says she'll be sweeping her way through life, protecting minor life forms."

"As well as sweeping one's path so as not to step on a bug," he informed, trying for a chatty, un-pedantic tone, "the more ascetic Jains wear a white cloth over their mouths so as not to breathe in living organisms." Thus Emerson scoured his mind for Jain minutiae.

"That would match her white debutante dress. Do you think she's still a virgin?"

"Yes."

Emma snorted a dainty laugh. "All fathers think their daughters are virgins."

"The more ascetic Jains don't wear clothes," he persisted, still trying to recoup his loss about the Islam business. "They call it wearing the sky."

"How pretty." She finished her drink and said, "Hinduism?" making it a question as if she were still deferring to his greater knowledge.

"Yes."

"Can you help me a little?"

"Zoroastrianism."

"Good heavens what a mouthful. We can thank God for small blessings that she didn't become one of those. I'm going for another lemonade and a sweater."

Emma left the porch and Nell took her place. "I've been listening in," she said. "Don't worry. I'm not going to do anything extreme, although I will only go to a college where I can learn Sanskrit. I just want to live a virtuous life of nonviolence, speaking the truth, never stealing, being celibate, and shunning worldly wealth. Those are the five great vows on the path of self-realization. I shall, of course, be vegetarian, but Jain women can't be sky-clad."

"Also, as a Jain," Emerson said contentedly, "women cannot obtain enlightenment without first being reborn as men."

"I'm not sure that's true nowadays but I could always transgender myself."

"I forbid you to transgender. It's bad enough that you have to give up sex and killing—two of life's great pleasures."

"Phooey. You're the most nonviolent man I know. I think you're a secret Jain. After all, it was your book that showed me the way."

"Shinto!" Emma shouted from within. "That's five."

Damn, thought Emerson, another non-*ism.*

"Seven!" Nell shouted back then muttered to her father, "She can't even count."

"Don't disrespect your mother." How many times had he said that over the years? He felt downhearted at Nell's behavior toward her mother and also at Shinto's non-*ism*-ness, although he seemed to remember that it was also acceptably known as Shintoism. He appreciated Emma's delicacy of retreating to another room before she pounced so that his defeated face would not be on display. Nell wouldn't notice.

Nell said, "I will disrespect her slave-block ritual of Coming Out. *Here's this pretty virgin all in white, for sale to the richest, most socially prominent suitor.* Give me a break."

"It's only a party, Nell. I believe this whole Jain escapade is just to avoid the Debutante Cotillion."

"If I got started on my transgendering right now, I could definitely avoid it."

Morgan joined them carrying a strange-hued cocktail. He was totally drunk. Nell looked at him with awe. Here was a person who honestly didn't care about anything or anyone. Pure detachment. She felt he was already enlightened.

He smiled at her sloppily and said nothing. He never talked when he was drunk, just sat there loose-limbed and sweet. She and Emerson fell silent also. From within the house, Emma shouted, "Debutantism!" and the two men smiled while Nell rolled her eyes.

"Jain is the most nonviolent of all the religions," said Nell, taking up the conversational reins. "All the others have launched armies at one time or another, even Buddhists. I know that for the rest of my life people will be asking me: 'What would you do if someone threatened your child with violence? Would you just stand there and look peaceful?' It's too tiresome."

"Just kill the people who ask you that," Emerson suggested. "Exasperating people aren't really living organisms or sentient beings."

Emerson and Nell breathlessly watched Morgan bring the stemmed cocktail glass in a slow, wavering motion to his lips, then released their breaths when he drank successfully. He replaced the glass on the table, closed his eyes, let his torso fall onto the chair, thence into a roll to the porch floor and a recumbent repose.

With perfect timing, Emma arrived with a blanket and covered him from head to toe. "Good. He won't be driving tonight." She looked hauntingly at Nell, clasping her hands to her heart. "If only *he* had decided to be a Jain. Then I could stop fearing for his life and the lives of others at his hands."

Was this the root of her haunted eyes and trembling hands? Nell wondered. She was stunned at her mother's desperate passion, a *mother's* passion she suddenly realized. She blurted out, "Mommy, is Morgan your son?"

She saw her parents look at each other. "He is, isn't he? I am utterly confused."

Emma took Nell's hand. "I was your father's mistress, darling, when he was married to his first wife, and she took Morgan to raise as I couldn't then. Morgan doesn't know. He loves the woman he believes to be his mother."

"But then you are all living a lie!" Nell wanted to wrench her hand away from her mother's grasp, but it felt so good where it was. "It's not right conduct. You should tell him. You must tell him."

Silence again until Emma, never one to be confrontational said, "Buddhism, that's eight."

How could her mother change this momentous subject with this silly great-religion count? "That's not fair," Nell protested. "You were listening in when I said about Buddhism being war-like."

"But, darling, this family always listens in, and aren't we helping each other to discover the entire ten?"

"Even those on floors under blankets listen in," came a slurry voice from the floor. "But I already knew."

"About Buddhism?" Emma asked.

He measured his words. "Children always know. Especially those who look exactly like their real mother. How does a small, dark, child come from two tall blue-eyed blonds? Do you think I'm an idiot?"

"Forgive us for not telling you," Emma said.

"Forgive me for…" he began, then closed his eyes.

Forgive him for what? Nell wondered. Causing her mother's hands to tremble? All this was making her big decision about becoming a Jain seem negligible. It was Nell's turn to sulk.

Nell and her parents watched a bug crawl laboriously across the floor tiles.

"Please do return it eventually," Emma told Nell, who frowned at the way her mother leaped airily from subject to subject no matter how enthralling the present one.

"Return what?" she asked grumpily.

Emma leaned over, puckered her mouth, and blew the bug to safety under the porch couch. "My book about Jain," she said. "My guiding light."

"*Your* book?" Nell quavered. "Your guiding light?"

"Yes, Nell darling, and by the way, the last two are…."

"Confucianism," said Emerson, raising his glass.

"And," said Morgan, raising himself, "Taoism."

"Taoism," Nell said simultaneously. They all smiled.

My Wings

Olivia Fisher-Smith, Grade 8

My hands:
a bit of my father on my mother's figure.

My hair:
a river during a storm.

My eyes:
two sisters with different faces.

My feet:
driftwood on a rocky shore.

My words:
a tumbling waterfall.

My thoughts:
a galloping horse.

My dreams:
a happy almost-real.

My mind:
wings on a baby bird
waiting to be used
and rise above the forest floor.

Clare Elsaesser, *Flower Child*, 2013, acrylic on watercolor paper, 10 × 8 inches

Chicken Crossings

Judy Brackett

JOE'S FAVORITE pastime, besides running around the farmyard with Dog and Hinnypinny or climbing the cottonwoods along the creek or trying to ride the old bike, is sitting at the top of the stairs, watching and listening to the uncles below at the big round table covered with the blue-and-red-bandana tablecloth that the aunties made. The uncles drink coffee, sip cider or whiskey, and talk, talk, talk. They are readers, thinkers, singers, storyspinners, joketellers.

Today Joe, who's four, sits up there with Hinnypinny on his lap. She's two and has blue legs and lays blue eggs—an Ameraucana, she's one of Joe's best friends, along with Dog and Pinochle the horse. Sometimes Dog sits with Joe and Hinnypinny. The horse is not allowed in the house.

The uncles have pretty well finished with what's wrong with the gov'ment and the farm bureau, and with the way McGee insists on laying out his crops east-west when every farmer worth his John Deere knows north-south is way better, and their voices lighten to songs, jokes, and other philosophies.

Uncle Victor says, "René Descartes walks into a bakery. Baker asks him if he'd like a croissant. Descartes says, 'I think not,' and vanishes."

"Good one," says Vincent, but he's not laughing. Joe doesn't get it.

Joe doesn't get most of their talk or their jokes, but he loves the rise and fall of the voices, the interruptions and merriment. Once,

Emmeline Craig, *Laundry in the wind with green hills,* 2007, watercolor on paper, 10¾ × 8½ inches

Victor laughed so hard he fell off his chair. Auntie May said the single malt maybe had something to do with that.

Vincent says, "If red fox slinks through the alfalfa toward the coop and nobody sees or hears him, maybe he's not really there. Maybe he won't get to the chickens tonight."

Joe sits up tall and clutches Hinnypinny.

"Depends," says Victor, and he takes a sip of his halfmilk-halfcoffee. "Some critter's likely out there—owl, bat, garter snake. They'd hear, so, yessir, fox is there. He *will* get into the henhouse."

Vincent says, "Hmmm. Speaking of chickens, d'you know what Emily Dickinson said when a little girl visitor asked her, 'Why'd the chicken cross the road?'"

Joe knows that one, and he pipes up, "To get to the other side!" and the uncles chuckle.

Victor says, "Nope. Because he could not stop for death, of course." Joe doesn't get that one, either.

Vincent asks, "What did Hemingway say about why the chicken crossed the road?"

Victor shakes his head. "Dunno."

"To die. In the rain. Alone."

The uncles are silent, then Victor says, "Isn't that just the saddest thing."

Joe hugs Hinnypinny tighter, trying to think of a real joke. Whenever he and the uncles and their friends stand around at the gas station, it's always a happy time—weather-and-crops talk, laughter, jokes, good-natured teasing.

Joe pokes his head between the balusters. "I know a good joke!" The uncles crane their necks and look at him.

Joe stands and Hinnypinny flaps off his disappearing lap, floats-flies to the floor below, hops across the room, cluckedy-clucking out the door, and disappears around the corner.

Taking a deep breath, Joe says, "Gas station!" The uncles wait for more, and Joe repeats, "Gas station! Gas station!"

And the uncles break into laughter as Joe sings it out again and again. The aunties bustle in. "What's the fuss? What's the fuss?" So Joe tells them his joke, and they laugh, too. Now Victor bends over, lifts a tablecloth red ruffle, and dabs at his eyes.

Auntie Rose shakes her head and turns back to the kitchen, then hollers over her shoulder, "Gas station!" and the laughter rises again.

Joe giggles, stands on tiptoe, swoops a leg over the railing, and slides down to join them.

Living with a Ghost

Burt Bacharach, Autograph Musical Manuscript

LYRICS BY STEVEN SATER

BURT BACHARACH

Prod. ______ **Title** Ghost **Page** 1

Arranger ______

JUDY GREEN MUSIC Hollywood, CA 90028 (213) 466-2491 PS-1325

From the musical, *Some Lovers*

BURT BACHARACH

Prod. ______ Title Ghost ______ Page 2

Arranger ______

Em — Em D — [C] G Bridge — Gmaj7

For some hymn to his mind — As he leaves you behind — And the you're waitin — Like that

25 26 27 28 29 30 31 32

Gmaj7 — Cm add 2 — Cm add 2 Cm — Am — Em — G

pointing — the scream — As he pockets your — pain for his stash — Still you

33 34 35 36 37 38 39 40

G — Gmaj7 — Cmaj7 — Am — Em

Know that — he's never gonna — wake from that dream

41 42 43 44 45 46 47 48

BURT BACHARACH

Prod. ____________ **Title** Ghost **Page** 3

Arranger ____________

opt Xtra Bar

Tenderly same tempo

Am 9 D 9/6 /A Am 9

Em

But then why would he look Back when he's got the whole world

49 50 51 52 53 54 55

Back to [A]

Still to catch

56 57 58

The Girl who sang my songs insert all 3 X

Bar 52 now becomes

Dmaj7 Dmaj7 C7sus C7 res

Back to [A]

Kinda rocked my world that—

with vigor

52 53 54 55

JUDY GREEN MUSIC Hollywood, CA 90028 (213) 466-2491 PS-132S

Novel Made of Haiku

Howard Norman

Just a lovesick fool / waiting for a persimmon / to ripen and fall. A white egret / rides atop a train / in the darkness. Listening to the radio concert / a crow / tilts its head. Despite a thousand poets / describing it / the moon is still beautiful. Passing clouds / never took a stone / from the mountain peak. Father and son / do repairs on / different squid boats. Two books of poetry / bookends / to a third. His daughter / reads a love letter / after cleaning fish. First snow / the snail / unafraid.

The inventor Suigaku / lends his friend a contraption / to cross the Milky Way.

I'll clean your lanterns / but can't pay / the debt I owe. Why would the fox / steal / only one shoe. Winter apricot / please / don't feel lonely. Woodpecker / thinks diagonally / is the only way to fly. Underside of leaves / keep secrets / for centuries. Even a cuckoo / looks solemn / in the temple. My feet look / different than this morning / in the bath. Kimonos of / my dead aunts / on the clothesline. On its way to the Capital / tortoise stops for a meal / after one step. Playing hooky / takes her calligraphy brush / to the movie matinee. Black leggings / always in fashion / for the cranes. Travelling toad / doesn't bend / a single bamboo stalk. "Put me up for the night?" / the snowy ditch / says yes. A monk / averts his eyes / from a festival dancer. Fool thinks / the spring ducks / will give love advice.

Madame Alvida Turns a Card

Lynn Hoggatt

MADAME ALVIDA has parked her caravan at the corner of Denfert Rochereau and the boulevard General Leclerc for as long as some people in the neighborhood can remember. It's a nineteen-fifties model in two-toned plastic, with aluminum windows and nothing remarkable about it except for its location and a sign, twenty centimeters by ten, swinging over the door. "MEDIUM," the sign reads across the top, in sharp white strokes. In the middle: a white hand on blue, with a circle in the palm, and below, "TAROT" in red. Two steps have been prised out of the metal frame below the door, where they now rest on the cobblestones in a swirl of brown and yellow leaves.

A wind is blowing along with the cars speeding into the rue Froidevaux, and it keeps going while the cars line up at the light by the graveyard. However, Madame Alvida is open for business in spite of the wind. Madame Alvida is open for business whenever the metal stair is in place, the appearance of which has nothing whatever to do with the weather and nothing to do with the traffic, but is tied to the phase of the moon and the signals she has been dreaming. Or so the neighbors are forced to assume, for she doesn't keep regular hours, which doesn't seem to discourage her customers, but rather, adds to her charm. "Ah! Madame Alvida is in today!" people say. "Assuredly, now is the time to touch the *beyond*."

On this particular morning, though Madame's metal stair says "In," today she is out of sorts. A young officer, new to the district, of course, and with nothing better to do, has just beat a hasty retreat after first tapping heavily on her window and then meeting the scorn in her sharp old eyes with a prickling, cold recoil. Yes, she has her license, of course—and holds it up. Now go away, go away! Unless you are waiting to be told a thing you don't want to hear! She chuckles as she recalls his silly face shrinking under the stiff, new, self-important cap as she says the words, and immediately feels better. Of course she would not have harmed him for the world—he is clearly not very bright—but these young Frenchmen have no respect. In Spain, he would not have dared rattle the window like that before she had finished her coffee, but she has been here twenty years now, and she knows how it is. It was worse under Franco, of course, but not wanting to stir that up, she busies herself at the paraffin stove with the kettle and straightens the tablecloth.

Madame Alvida's caravan has a red rug on the floor. It is thick and warm and altogether friendly to her feet in the deepening winter cold. On the table is a candle, on the wall a picture of three grandchildren sitting in swimsuits on the Costa Brava. On a shelf, next to a tarnished silver cross, a ceramic urn holds a fistful of incense tied with a purple ribbon. She mutters something, strikes a match, and slowly lights the candle, then, extracting a single stick, carefully reties the ribbon. Holding the stick to the flame, she removes it as soon as it begins to smoke, blowing on the reddening end and gently inserting it into her metal rose. These small movements are made with reverence, a ritual grace, and though no customer is present to be impressed, Madame Alvida does not consider depriving the spirits of their due.

Except for the lighting of candles, the daily tasks of organizing herself in this life have grown irksome to Madame, for, having been exposed to the consequences over the years and as often blamed for the foolish choices of her clients, she has lost patience with a great many common human failings. Indeed, not to hone too fine a point on Madame Alvida's temperament, she is an irascible old creature who expects the people tripping up her stair to be childishly dependent, and acts accordingly.

Few people, then, can bring themselves to like her, though if she is seldom treated to affection, she is unquestionably regarded with respect. In the neighborhood, it is even rumored that people from outside suffer long, jostling hours coming and going on the Metro to consult her on matters of importance, a thing no Parisian tolerates without reason. A leading politician was once thought to have been seen slipping down the metal stair, ashen-faced and bowed, but no one dares confirm it, for if Madame Alvida is not kind, she is equally not malicious, and the privacy of her clientele is ferociously sacrosanct.

It is altogether rare for anyone to bear the cost and tedium in legal stamps and forms of maintaining a mystical caravan in such a public place, so rumor may not lie when it supposes that Madame Alvida has been modestly successful in worldly terms. Still, this morning as she sits at the little deal table, she begins to feel morose. Her shoulders twitch, and something presses on the back of her neck. She scratches, then straightens up, sighs and leans back. There, embraced by the invisible, welcomed as a lover, all her sadness passes, and she closes her eyes, suddenly joyful, for Madame Alvida is among those rarest of seers, who read in the arms of the Most Beloved Friend. She never vacates or empties for possession, as some do, letting the riffraff in. Indeed, Madame Alvida puts up with all the rest only for this, and if she is difficult, she is also inspired, and the dueling aspects of her experience create the tension through which important things may be understood.

The wind continues to blow and the leaves to rush along, horns and voices to sound, but for a brief and precious time the old woman remains oblivious, relaxed in her chair, drawing in a sustenance without which she would long ago have given up. "I wanted to be a teacher," she told her granddaughter once, "but Most Beloved told me to give like this, and so the cards, and so the caravan, and so it is…."

Madame has always known she doesn't need the cards. They seem to reassure people, so she pretends to look but sees past them down to particulars. On dim days, the cards may act as windows to frame her responses, but when she is very clear the cards completely disappear and she witnesses the whole thing in flashes.

This morning she is held deeply by those angelic arms, and after a while she shakes herself, opens her eyes and begins to fix her hair, peering keenly into a mirror hung on a nail inside the cupboard. Madame's hair is long and white, rolled at the temples and attached in a knot at the top of her head with great bands of black shooting out from the roots. She arranges the pins with care and considers. Her forehead is still unlined, rising proudly under the coils of hair, and she wonders how this has come to be so, for she spends such a great deal of time concentrating on her brow that she imagines it should be tired by now, but it looks the youngest part of her and she shrugs. At eighty-two, she has come to accept things as they are.

Madame Alvida adjusts the flounces on her skirt and comes to attention, sits up straighter. She expects he is almost to the corner by now. First feel is strong and heavy. He fancies he is alone, she thinks, and wonders how anyone can be so insensitive and at once so terribly gifted. His image blurs, and for an instant she sees double, two dark figures, twins, before they slip back into one. Why? Then, with a jolt, she senses he can see her as she sees him. She opens her eyes to clear her mind by staring at the candle. Why is he coming to her, then? She perceives he is subject to influences and has blind spots, that is the reason, so sees she will have to be careful, and then she knows, or thinks she knows, why, before he goes double again.

He raps impatiently at the door and enters before she can call out, but she is ready. In he strides and stops. It seems a weight is massed at the door, of distilled thought or intention that is in no way inimical, but alert, discerning, and as he drops his gaze to her level, the faint sound of a distant concussion falls upon his ear and dissipates. Before him sits a small, upright figure in a plush, velvet chair; two bright eyes stare unblinkingly into his own, and the candle flame flutters. She holds his gaze in hers for longer than is customary. This is not about good manners, and her candle may do what it likes, but she is too old to flutter even in the presence of such a man, though something in her quickens. He probes coldly, incisively, but she doesn't shrink, and finding no trace of fear in her he stands back, uncertain, for he is not accustomed to fearlessness and it confuses him. He is sufficiently discomfited to remain wordlessly staring until, with a slight inclination of the head, she asks him to sit down. Again, she wonders how a man with the Gift can remain ignorant of what she sees around him, but so it is, and she registers his blindness as a tool in her hands for her use.

He is dark-haired with lightning streaks of white, and tall, with legendary shoulders. She thinks of Oriental satraps and looks deeper, fights through the man's fixation until it glitters and implodes. Something passes with furious intention, phosphorescent in the dark. She imagines the shadows of another life amidst the shining—a wild young man with a tender heart and a taste for dissipation—before being tugged in another direction, carried on a brightness. A rush of wings fills her inner ear, and something amorphous begins to shape itself. A chill comes over her as it comes over him. Something edges in. Again, the winds spark pictures, and she sees he wants to spurn the bottle, the powder, and the smoke. She perceives power of a kind and more determination than has ever been poised on the hard wooden chair in front of her. Willpower. Madame respects this, though it will not be enough to take him all the way home.

Anna Dal Pino, *Investigation of a Raven Investigating Me,* 2012, charcoal on paper, 10 × 14 inches

---

Perversely, she suddenly wants a cigarette and acknowledges her weak spot, distracted, then thinks with a measure of gratitude that human failings may save us from errors of greater magnitude once they are admitted. She doesn't ask his name, it doesn't matter. "I won't read the cards for you," she says, "I know what you want, and you know I can tell you like this. But I may ask questions."

"Good," he nods. "Go on."

"Wait," she insists, holding up her hand.

What she sees next are two dead women, and then another three, dimly, behind those two. They are less and they are more. The numbers are symbolic, but she cannot divine it all. Two women standing behind him touch his shoulders, one on each side, dividing him. The mother is distinctly outlined in red and pulling hard. The other is shrouded in the long grey smear of overdose. He holds to her holding as she holds, and neither can let go. Fixed on his shoulder, she squeezes and he shudders, leans back and breathes where it hurts and thrills him all the same, lets his body talk. "Don't let go," it says. "Don't let go."

Madame dislikes the picture, especially the drug dead. He needs no drugs there with her now. Their connection is frenzy enough and just as deadly. Shake it out, she tells herself, that righteous indignation. Judgments have no part in seeings of this kind; they only confuse what is. Madame sighs at the blasted waste of it.

The third woman, though, the one on this side? and the others behind her? How is it that he does not see this one when the mother and the drug dead he sees as clearly as any living being on the street? Something is as innocent as lambs though he has caught their hearts to himself, like flying stars, for her, trapped and put them into boxes, where they belong to him but beat for release, and the putting away of those hearts, in this way, in him, is like stepping over shards of glass in a broken street. His windows are dark, shattered, but Drug Dead is insatiable, and every single one of them that he takes down that way makes her stronger.

She lights another stick of incense and brings her hands together as if in prayer, raises them to her lips, looks down, then obliquely up. "What about Sibyline?" Her words snake across the candlelight and curl into smoke, but the man might not have heard them, for the stony set of his face doesn't shift. Slowly, he decides to respond, fully in control, dimples, then laughs. "I rarely called her that," he begins, "and only when she got pretentious. She knew less than she thought she did, and now she is mine for good."

"For good?" Madame whispers. "And who possesses whom? Don't you ever wonder?" But she has heard enough and gestures that this will do. May my will not be done on earth, she thinks with a regretful shudder. It is the age-old problem, the struggle between arrogance and gratitude, the terrible hunger for sensation when the spirit cannot rise. There is only one story and endless variations on the theme, but the man interrupts her thought.

"Have a cigarette," he suggests with a wink, and mocks, "if it will help you concentrate. Don't mind me." Now it is her turn to smile, for he has misjudged her as she knew he must. She shakes her head, again holding up her hand, and he subsides, having made his point, and she declines to inquire further of him for the moment, knowing he imagines he has come for entertainment, confirmation at most, thinking how far he has underestimated the forces that enmesh him. She turns her thoughts back to the matter at hand.

Again, she sees the images move out of the dark, like smoke, and as she watches, the man and his dead disappear. She opens a door in a rock and enters the dream of a stranger, a fresh-faced young woman who is walking under a grey light along an open hillside. Suddenly, a lion lunges past her, leaps into the bush and drags out the skinned carcass of an animal.

She has never done it before, but right then Madame decides to stake her all. She acts with clear purpose and no regret. To do so is not in keeping with the rules of her profession, and it will transform her own position permanently, but she does not hesitate. There is that about the young walker that shines and calls for sacrifice. Firmly, she inserts her will as a voice into the dream. "Run downhill," she commands. "Relinquish the field. Do not obstruct." As she says these words, she feels her own life is weighed in the balance until the young woman hears, until she turns and begins to run, and as she runs, the scale goes up/comes down. One life is forfeit and another saved, while the beast at the top of the hill continues to feed.

Madame is about to come back when her attention is drawn to the bottom of the hill, where the man who sits before her in her caravan lies weeping in the dream. His head is cradled in the lap of the dreamer, the woman who ran, and they are surrounded by a light Madame does not understand and does not attempt to explain. Addendums of this kind unsettle her.

At last, Madame tidies her mind on the candle flame and clears her throat, and when she speaks it is softly.

"A woman's love for you will not keep you from your destiny," she begins. "You will obtain that which you most desire, that which has been set before you. You will be welcomed to feast at the king's table. Feast you will, and feast well, in splendor, while at your side the shadow woman stands ready. You will have a choice that may allow you to enter that kingdom together and take the longest road." Then she cocks her head, looks at him quizzically, and surprises herself. "You know," she repeats slowly, "you will have a choice."

For a moment, the man regards her in silence, then asks, "What is the warning?"

"Remember," she says steadily, "that at a feast it is well to consider one's desserts."

"Ha!" he laughs, as though at a pleasantry, delighted. "You are playful. This means I will have a wonderful time and the last course will be the best," and he throws up his hands. He rises and gently places two crisp notes on the table by her candle, bows and departs. As though it had all been a game, she thinks, as easy as that. She closes her eyes and listens to his footsteps, then listens to the street, and high above the traffic noise she thinks she hears the wind, where blown through her eyes, she watches what will happen.

She is almost amused to learn that her visitor thinks he is a count, for counts and kings are not what they think they are, and that he will break a promise because of what she has just seen in the smoke. Then, again, in some ways the count is a bad listener, because he has spent a lifetime learning things few people have understood and thinks that makes him invincible. So he will go to a party with a well-known model pinned to his arm, an accessory to the fact. The woman, who hangs there breathlessly, he will not much desire, for she is empty of challenge for him, while the one he is currently stalking, a woman of heart, will wake up without him that morning, having comprehended through her dream, and so escape. The model will blow off like feathers and come to no harm, light as light, and for a little while the count will be bewildered, wondering how he has lost them both, and neither woman will know how close she has come to falling under the sway of a petty tyrant who imagines he is free.

There is a darkness still owing, a family debt of which he is ignorant, cadavers not his own, and some that are—bones of spirit, blood, and flesh. She does not understand the light at the end of her dream, but she is not Almighty and she does not have to know. She just has to finish her task. Madame has always known how to reckon up the costs, and she begins to tally. She will pay with good grace and not grumble, for she is tired and the count has wasted enough. She sees a brighter sphere and new shoots under starlight. It will be all right, and although Madame is not given to sentimentality, she softens and smiles to herself.

She is rolling her first cigarette of the day when the play of shadow and light and the click of a sharp heel on stone announce another visitor, and into the story steps the girl in the dream, unsought that morning, and unforeseen.

Vagrant

Margaret Stawowy

In ornithology, a bird that has strayed off its usual migration route.

Not the first bird
with cuckoo clockwork
to misalign a star,
to take a dyslexic turn at Denver,
and descend

to a grove by an ocean not so pacific.
Specifically, these trees don't belong here either:
cypress, eucalyptus, transplanted
by someone in love
with anomaly, with what shouldn't be,

but is. Out on a limb, the odd
bird alights and roosts in the wrong
picture. Puzzle pieces
of land and sea don't fit
the width of its instinct. If

only it could fly backward,
row the air to a line in the atmosphere,
that place passed by mistake
where its compass whirs
unbent. But here

is the ocean unrolling into an upside
down sky, licking air, swallowing the blood
orange horizon. There is no Mexico
out here, no place to land,
no place at all.

Kerry Livingston, *Blackbirds over the Wetlands*, detail from an eight-panel quilt titled *Our Wild Story*, 2011, linen cloth and embroidery thread, 10 × 10 inches

Traditional Botanical Paintings

Claudia Stevens

(Opposite) *California Thistle* (Cirsium occidentale), 2013, watercolor and gouache, 18 × 22 inches; (above) *Sand Bottlebrush* (Beaufortia squarrosa), 2013, watercolor and gouache, 18 × 22 inches

(Opposite) *Sticky Monkey Flower* (Mimulus aurantiacus), 2013, watercolor and gouache, 18 × 22 inches; (above) *California Buckeye* (Aesculus californica), 2013, watercolor and gouache, 18 × 22 inches

Elders

Florence Caplow

AS A BOTANIST, for years I wanted to travel to the land of the old Great Basin bristlecone pines, *Pinus longaeva*, in the White Mountains of California. The most ancient trees on the planet are there, in a remote, arid, cold world above ten thousand feet. A youngster bristlecone pine might be a thousand years old, and the oldest known to date, named the "Methuselah Tree," is nearly five thousand years old, which means that this tree germinated about the time that civilization began. Individual needles on these trees can last for eighty years or more—the lifespan of a human being, if we're lucky.

In May of 2006 I was finally able to make my pilgrimage to these elders. From the hot, dry floor of the Owens Valley I drove up and up, through a canyon filled with wildflowers, into scrubby, piñon pine and juniper forests. Then as if on to the roof of the world, I drove along a road that skirted the edge of steep slopes overlooking the Sierra to the west, the sun glinting off snowfields fifty miles away. The Sierra Mountains catch most of the rainfall that comes to California from the Pacific, so the White Mountains are cold and very dry, a desert atop a mountain range. The ground is mostly rock here above nine thousand feet, with flowers nestled in and among the rocks and scattered, wind-shaped trees.

At the end of the road, high above the tree line of juniper and piñon pine, where only the dense, sculpted cushion plants of the true alpine should grow, is the bristlecone forest, standing in this place since the last Ice Age.

I had camped nearby and arrived early, so I had the four-mile trail to the most ancient trees of the Methuselah Grove to myself. The light had a too-bright, almost surreal quality, reflecting off the white dolomite rock, bouncing off a dark blue sky, and the elevation made walking harder than I expected. The silence was intense: no bird calls, no rustling in the branches, not even the sound of the wind. Just my footsteps and quick breaths in the thin air.

The pines around me were short, broad, impossibly gnarled, perhaps thirty feet high, with roots thrust into what seemed like bare rock and trunks nearly bleached white. The limbs of the older trees were mostly dead. Only narrow strips of chestnut-colored bark supported a few short, living branches contorted into wild, spiraling shapes. Bristlecones can't be separated from the wind or the cold that shape them—they are the shape of the wind of the White Mountains. They are like the faces of very old people, which come to show every nuance of character. To call them beautiful would be accurate but somehow shallow. They're a little scary, far beyond conventional grace. They occupy a realm of absolute originality.

Bristlecones manifest the idea that adversity can have advantages. These trees survive in some of the most adverse conditions in the world: a three-month growing season, howling winds for months at a time, bitter cold, constant dryness, and periodic severe drought. And yet the evolutionary history of the tree in concert with these conditions creates a kind of perfection, and surely perfection is not too strong a word for a plant that's found a way to live for the last eleven thousand years in the same place. The dryness and cold, and the trees' infinitesimally slow growth rate, create wood that is nearly impervious to insects or rot. When a tree is hit by lightning, only a part of the tree dies; the rest stays alive on a slender ribbon of cambium. Because they live so long, each bristlecone needs only one viable offspring every few thousand years to keep the population going.

The Methuselah Grove lies in a sheltered fold beneath the high ridgelines, saturated with bright desert light. Here the trees go beyond maturity into something else entirely. Some trees have been growing so long in one place that the ground has eroded out from beneath them, and their massive roots are exposed for many feet beyond the base of the tree, as twisted as the branches above them. Some trees are many feet in diameter but have only one small living strip of bark and a single branch still very much alive. On the rocky ground are dead tree trunks—some have been lying there for seven thousand years or more. Imagine living for thousands of years, then finally dying and staying upright for a thousand years or more before toppling over, to remain indefinitely with everyone you've ever known!

I sat down at the base of one of the big trees. I tried to comprehend that I sat among living beings that had been alive for a hundred times my lifetime—and that some had been dead for twice that long. I wanted to feel the shiver of vast time, but instead what I felt was the degree to which I was bound by the narrow confines of my own perspective. I felt like a flea that can't imagine what it would be like to be a dog, and to live for years rather than days.

So this is what it's like to be a human being, with a human lifespan, I thought, in my flea-like way. We have powerful imaginations, which can, at times, allow us to believe that we have entered the experience of another, but fundamentally, the world we see and experience is the world shaped by our own perceptions.

As I write this, many months later, I think of the bristlecones, still standing in that high place, holding their twisted branches up to the dark blue sky, expressing in their silence a nearly infinite dignity. We'll always be fleas and seedlings by comparison—a young, short-lived, often foolish species—but I hope we have the capacity to stand in our little lives with dignity, as they do; perhaps we, too, can grow to be elders, living with grace in the storms of the world.

Britta Kathmeyer, *Gossip,* 2013, smoke, ink, and pencil on paper, 11 × 14 inches

Sarah Myers, *Polka Dot Pathogen,* 2013, beet juice and sumi ink on paper, 17 × 14 inches

First Miwok Poem

Carolyn Losee

ewe mu kuleyis
potola-ko mulu
saka uti
uti hi ka

uunumt hoipus ka
unu wea kole-mulu
yemi kik, liwa
yoa muluta

henalupu yawemuki
kal, kitcau hianahitis
wenetumai talawalanta
koto hiana

milk-breasted woman showing
whiteman's head
how you cradle your child
through the small sun door

in the large chief's house
mother of earth-colored hair
sweeps ashes, sprinkles water
upon the dirt floor

windrock and snowfire
smoke, blood and daystars streak
medicinewood and thunder arrows
across the grasshoppered dawn

Flash Fiction in Two Parts

Frances Lefkowitz

I. FORSYTHIA

FATHER, DOCTOR, husband—it doesn't matter who tells me what to do to get better slept, I'm not going to do it. One wants me to get a pet, another says lay off the caffeine, stop reading the newspaper. Look, the window for advice is closed. Go reveal to yourself your own secret tricks. Maybe I want to be up all night, despite my lack of pep the next day. Maybe the radio is better late than early. Maybe dancing in my socks to obscure songs that don't get daytime airplay is as good a way to spend my time as any other. Maybe you shouldn't watch if it chafes you to see me jello around the house jiggling at the blending of my desperation with raw guitar chords and oozing voices from a bygone era. The men in my life, including my son, who I now must count among the men, only want the best for me. But the worst has happened—I lost my mother without making up—and the best shrivels at the prospect of trying to protect me from this. A fact is a rare, rare thing, with so many angles of opinion and interpretation. But death is like math, even more irrefutable. Keep peeling and you will find no other version, nothing fruitier, nothing perfumier, nothing you'd want to plant in your garden among the forsythia to bloom defiantly first thing next spring. Yet this is exactly what I've done, in the middle of the night, which is my night now, with a flashlight and the gritty ashes. And when those bare branches yell in yellow at the remnants of snow in early April, I will kneel before them and say I'm sorry. Then maybe, just maybe, I will get some sleep.

II. SCORPIO

IN THE SKY, a scorpion, its tail coiled around the western hemisphere, its chest arching toward the Pacific. In the water, microbes created starbursts wherever we broke the surface with our paddles. Black and electric above and below us, we floated like astronauts in the giddy elements, twirling in circles, completely succumbing to the spectacle. Then the fog came in and erased our merrymaking, along with Scorpio and the other guides. This is how it is with sea and

Kerry Livingston, *Singing by Firelight*, detail from an eight-panel quilt titled *Our Wild Story*, 2011, linen cloth and embroidery thread, 10 × 10 inches

space: the invigorating magic that makes you feel so alive suddenly changes and leaves you stranded. Only when we couldn't see did we remember that we'd forgotten the flashlight, the compass, the Band-Aids, the whiskey, all back at his house. I tried to maintain my cool, but did question his judgment and therefore my own, for choosing him. We selected direction by scent and guesswork, first his, then mine, then his again. Everything he ever said came back to me, but I had to focus away from him if I wanted to get us to land. It turned out he had us headed north, out of the bay, almost into the ocean. When the current picked up, tried to carry us to wherever Scorpio was pointing, we stopped bickering, dug in. Now that we knew where south was, we worked our bodies to get there. When it was all over, and we'd beached our boats almost exactly where we'd put in, he wanted to run on the sand, to sing and yelp at the hidden moon, to get naked and push his cold flesh into me. He had almost died several times before and always it lifted him. But I longed for old reliable things: a tattered but sturdy hemp line, the ragged front seat of my car. He chattered, I shivered. We got back to the house, and I took the extra bed. In a few hours, solar would replace lunar, and the world would look different all over again.

Claudia Chapline, *New American Garden Book,* 2013, altered book, collage, shellac, 12½ × 16 × 5½ inches

Barbara Vos, *Spring Fed,* 2008, acrylic on paper, 60 × 72 inches

Machinery, Waiting

Tim Foley

ON A September morning in 2013, I drive from Sacramento to the prison at San Quentin to meet with a man sentenced to death. I cross the Richmond Bridge under a pale blue, late-summer sky. Mount Tamalpais rises before me.

Exiting the freeway, I drive past the cluster of houses known as San Quentin Village. A sign cautions me to drive slowly: "Children at Play." In all the years I have been coming here, I have never seen a single child, at play or otherwise, along this stretch of road leading to the prison.

San Quentin, the first and oldest of the California prisons, sits on a stunning piece of property alongside San Francisco Bay. The water laps against the edge of the visitor parking lot. Out of my car, I look east across the bay, a panorama that includes Red Rock Island and the hills of Alameda County. The forested hump of Angel Island lies to the south. To the southwest stretches the Tiburon Peninsula, a particularly exclusive part of Marin County. They say that if the wind is right, the sound of shouted cadences from the prison yard, drifting over the marina at Paradise Cay, can be heard in the yards of multi-million-dollar estates.

I lock the car, leaving my wallet and phone inside. I carry a folder containing legal papers and a notepad. I walk up the slope, mount a set of stairs, and go through a door into a long hallway that smells of moldy plaster and old paint. I leave my car key, with its prohibited computer chip, in a locker and place the locker key in a clear plastic baggie, which also contains coins and single dollar bills. Along with the baggie and my folder, I carry three pens and my identification. Nothing else.

There are rules regarding what a visitor can bring into a maximum security prison. No wallets, purses, satchels, or briefcases. No cell phones, tape recorders, or computers. No drugs or anything that might be used as a weapon. Clothing is restricted as well: no green (the color the guards wear), no denim (the material the prisoners wear), nothing revealing. I'm an attorney, and I dress the part: grey suit, white shirt, grey necktie.

Halfway down the hallway is the door leading into the processing center. On Saturdays and Sundays, this hallway is crowded with wives, girlfriends, children, the families of prisoners. But today is a weekday, and I am alone. A buzzing noise signals that the door has been unlocked and I step through.

Two guards run the processing room. One confirms my appointment at a computer. All visitors must be cleared in advance; first-timers are subject to a criminal records and immigration check. I received my clearance years ago. I've been representing death row inmates, and visiting San Quentin, for twenty-eight years. Some things have changed. Gone are the little slips on which we wrote the name and number of our client, and signed a waiver stating that the prison bore no responsibility should we be taken hostage. These have been replaced by the computer-generated, single-page print-out the guard hands me after he checks my folder and examines my plastic baggie of money.

A second guard oversees my trip through the metal detector and stamps my inside right wrist with a liquid that can only be seen under infrared light. I step out of the processing room and walk the three hundred yards down the roadway to the cellblocks. To my right, personnel buildings and the warden's office. To my left, the staff parking lot and, beyond, the waters of the bay shining in the morning sunlight. On the sidewalk, a painted orange-yellow line leads all the way to the main visiting room. I pass a guard tower and turn in front of the older, medieval-looking portion of the prison, "1890" painted between the windows of its third story. I pass the flagpole and the monument to the ten guards slain "in the line of duty" between 1952 and 1985, their names and dates of death carved in marble. Above me, visible over the roof of a red brick section of the prison, is a greenish, copper-coated exhaust pipe, a remnant of the days when cyanide gas was used to execute the condemned—and then expelled into the sky after its work was done.

I cross the roadway and step up to a sliding gate made of metal mesh reinforced with clear Plexiglas. The door hums as a motor engages, and the door slides open in a jerking, noisy fashion. I step through into a sallyport and, as the outer door grinds shut, hand my identification and appointment sheet through a slot in a Plexiglas window to a guard. When the guard is satisfied that all is as it should be, he flips a switch, and the inner gate ratchets open.

When I first met with death row inmates at San Quentin, visits took place in a large room on the ground floor of East Block. The room was an open area, with plastic chairs and tables. Along one wall were vending machines dispensing coffee, sodas, snacks, and microwaveable sandwiches. Along another wall was a raised platform with a desk and chair where one or two guards looked out over the room. On a third wall, between alcoves reserved for non-contact visits behind glass, an inmate artist had painted murals of mountain landscapes and peaceful domesticity. Lawyers met with their clients next to families visiting fathers or sons. Children laughed. Chess games were played.

Visitors chatted with one another and inmates exchanged greetings. Once, I sat a few feet away from a movie star who had engineered a visit with an inmate to research a role. The atmosphere, considering the circumstances, was not altogether oppressive. If you tried hard, you might imagine you were in the basement cafeteria of a low-rent office building or a mildly decrepit bus station waiting room.

Nowadays, contact visits with condemned men occur in one of eleven locked metal-and-Plexiglas cages. Most are the size of a closet, just large enough for a small table and two or three plastic chairs. The inmates are always shackled—handcuffed behind the back—in the presence of staff. They are escorted from the tiers, led to the assigned cage, and locked in with the visitor. Only then are the shackles removed, unlatched through a shoebox-sized slot in the door of the cage. These are the privileged inmates, allowed contact visits. Otherwise, it's all behind metal and Plexiglas, using a phone.

Back in the old East Block visiting room, you simply told the guard when your visit was over. Now, a strict schedule is enforced. Visits are set in ninety-minute blocks. If a visitor wants or needs more time and the slots are not full, a second ninety-minute block can be added on, but only by arrangement in advance. Cutting a visit short is difficult, as you have to flag down a staff member from inside the cage and hope the guard will be willing and able to depart from the set schedule.

The vending machines are still there, lined up across a walkway from the cages, inaccessible to inmates. Regular visitors go through a ritual of purchasing food and drink items, placing them on a plastic tray, and carrying them into the cage. I use my dollar bills and coins to purchase a can of Pepsi, a bag of Doritos, and a frozen burrito, which I heat up in an ancient microwave oven. I greet a few other lawyers who are buying snacks for their clients. I carry my tray to the cage I've been assigned for my visit.

As of mid-September 2013 there are 741 condemned inmates in California. The condemned women—twenty of them—are housed a couple of hundred miles away in a prison near Chowchilla. A handful of condemned inmates with acute medical problems are shipped temporarily to a facility in Vacaville. The rest, more than seven hundred men, sleep in cells in San Quentin not far from the execution chamber.

The state government took over executions from the counties in 1891, and San Quentin hosted its first hanging in 1893. In 1937, the preferred method of dispatching the prisoner changed from hanging to asphyxiation by cyanide gas, and a gas chamber was built in a corner of San Quentin. The original death row of the prison, a nearby corridor of cells, had a capacity of sixty-four inmates. For decades, no one could have imagined that the condemned population would ever need more space.

Today, East Block, five tiers high, with dozens of cells on each tier, holds hundreds of condemned inmates. Others, restricted for disciplinary reasons, live in a closely monitored section of the prison called the "Adjustment Center." Most of the condemned have been here a long time. Delays in the review of capital cases, caused by a lack of qualified and willing counsel, the workload of the appellate courts, and the size and complexity of cases, have reached absurd levels. Each of the last five inmates executed by California waited more than twenty years for imposition of judgment. Some current prisoners have been on the row for thirty. Attempts to speed up the system have failed. California is not Texas.

California has not executed a prisoner since early 2006. There is no single reason for what has become a de facto and unofficial moratorium on executions, but one significant factor is the botched manner in which the California Department of Corrections and

Rehabilitation transitioned from executions by cyanide gas to executions by lethal injection. Authorities clumsily converted the old gas chamber—an airtight, vacuum-sealed room with a sturdy chair anchored in the middle—by installing a slab with lengthy IV tubes that ran through an observation window into a dark side room more conducive to hiding the identity of the executioner than giving technicians enough light to properly mix and deliver the fatal three-drug "cocktail." Proper medical procedures were ignored, staff were untrained, and several executions were awkward and painfully long. Litigation ensued, and the CDCR reacted defensively, attempting to hide or excuse missteps. When independent medical experts were allowed to examine the situation, they were appalled. A federal judge shut the system down, declaring that the risk of an unnecessarily painful execution was too extreme to be tolerated.

Since then, the CDCR has built a completely new execution chamber at San Quentin, at a cost of $853,000, and issued new regulations and protocols for executing the condemned. Anti-death-penalty advocates complained that state transparency and administrative rules were violated, and a new wave of litigation occurred, further blocking attempts to resume executions.

In the meantime, California law still provides for death sentences, murders happen, and trial courts and juries still impose the ultimate punishment. Men, and the occasional woman, are added to the growing list. Since the beginning of 2012, twenty-six death judgments have been imposed in California. In the last five years, the list of condemned has grown by roughly one hundred.

Yet the list sometimes shrinks. A court case may result in the removal of a name, freedom for the wrongfully convicted, or a resentencing to something less than death. But, more often, the hangman is cheated by nature: an aging death row inmate, having waited more than a quarter-century for the government to kill him, succumbs to cancer or heart failure or stroke. Others lose hope and take their own lives. Since the last execution in California, forty condemned men have died from natural causes or suicide.

The cost of California's death penalty system is enormous. At every stage, capital cases are much more expensive than other felony cases. Three state agencies exist solely to process and monitor capital appeals and post-conviction litigation. Federal and state courts devote extensive resources to the appeals and post-conviction petitions. Capital defendants commonly have two publicly paid attorneys and are guaranteed the services of court-appointed counsel at all stages. California's death penalty system has, since 1978, added an estimated $4 billion to the cost of the state's criminal justice system. In that time "only" thirteen men have been executed by the state. The result, a 2011 study concluded, is "the perpetuation of a multibillion-dollar

Ryan Dunbar, Grade 11, Tomales High School, *Simple Complexity*, 2011, altered photograph

fraud on California taxpayers" and "a bloated system, in which condemned inmates languish on death row for decades before dying of natural causes."

The expense and futility of the system have changed the debate over the use of the death penalty from one of morality to one of utilitarianism, and converted supporters into opponents. The author of the 1978 initiative promulgating the law is now in favor of its repeal. Former California Chief Justice Ronald George, who came into prominence early in his career as a talented appellate advocate for the death penalty, has publicly declared California's system broken. A special state commission released a report in 2007 concluding that the dysfunctional administration of the death penalty creates "cynicism and disrespect for the law" while "increas[ing] the emotional trauma experienced by murder victims' families." Federal judge Arthur Alarcón, a former prosecutor who helped clear the way for executions as clemency secretary to Governor Pat Brown, has co-authored a series of articles sharply critical of the waste and cruelty of the California system of capital punishment, and announced that he believes "maintaining the status quo is intolerable."

Early in 2012, opponents of the death penalty qualified an initiative for the November ballot. Proposition 34 would have abolished the death penalty in California. Supporters stressed the wastefulness, expense, and futility of the system. Arguments founded on ethics were de-emphasized in favor of arguments based on fiscal responsibility.

History was against Proposition 34, however. In elections prior to 2012, California voters had consistently approved the death penalty by wide margins, and every time they had a chance to expand the reach of capital punishment, they did so—six consecutive times. By law, the modern death penalty in California can only be abolished by the voters, and the voters seem to like it. But the proponents of

Proposition 34 thought that circumstances and attitudes had changed. Their hope was bolstered when the supporters of capital punishment failed to fund an organized opposition.

Then, two months before election day, the *San Francisco Chronicle* ran a story revealing that a group of outspoken death row inmates were opposed to the initiative and were urging people to vote against it. While many capitally sentenced prisoners are mentally ill or incompetent, many others are interested and engaged in the legal issues involved in their appeals. Some write to reporters and politicians. Some file lawsuits and independent petitions challenging their convictions. Some ask the courts to fire their attorneys. And some parse Supreme Court opinions and follow legal developments with an understandable obsessiveness.

Death row inmates are special. All felony defendants are entitled to counsel at trial and during their first direct appeal, and will receive court-appointed and government-paid counsel if they cannot afford their own. Capitally sentenced prisoners, however, receive court-appointed counsel beyond the first appeal, all the way until execution of judgment. With the lawyers come visits, attention, letters, and sometimes quarterly packages and birthday presents. In addition, while doing time in East Block at San Quentin is difficult and frightening, it could be worse. Condemned prisoners are single-celled, while general population prisoners share their closet-sized living space with at least one other convicted felon. Inmates understand that doing time on death row at San Quentin in a one-man cell, with a relatively calm yard, a certain status, and lawyers and paralegals working on overturning convictions, can be a more desirable situation than doing life without parole, double-celled, forgotten, and unvisited, in a gang-infested institution like Folsom Prison.

The downside of death row for an inmate, of course, is that the government is trying to kill him and, once the appeals are finished, will.

Doing time on death row was never intended to be more desirable than ordinary prison time. But inmates know that there has not been an execution in more than seven years, and how long the old-timers have been on the row. They see the older men dying from cancer, not in a chamber surrounded by spectators. So many—not all, but many—do not fear execution. And so perhaps it is not entirely odd that some defendants, convicted of murder, see death row as the lesser horror of two dismal futures, and resist attempts to abolish the death penalty.

As, ultimately, did California voters: Proposition 34 failed. The final vote was 48 percent in favor and 52 percent opposed. Consequently, the "intolerable" situation continues. Fourteen condemned men have exhausted all court challenges and wait for execution dates, a list that will grow. Eventually, litigation over the method of execution will end and a new, presumably more efficient machinery of death will lurch forward.

My visit ends. Two guards come to shackle my client and walk him back to East Block. I wait for the signal that he has been cleared. In the sallyport, the guard hands me back my identification. I pass through the mechanical sliding gate and back along the orange-yellow line.

The midday sky is a deeper blue. The surface of the bay shines. I walk past a low-security inmate standing on a ladder painting a wall. I move through the processing center and retrieve the key to my car from the locker.

Back in the parking lot, I look south. The tower of the new eastern span of the Bay Bridge is silhouetted against the old bridge. The Larkspur ferryboat churns through the water. A cargo ship and tugboat move slowly across the bay.

Carolyn Krieg, *Red Deer,* 2013, archival pigment print

Zea Morvitz, (opposite) *Crossed Trunks*, 2011, graphite on Gampi Surface paper, 38 × 25 inches; (above) *Inverness Drawing #4*, 2011, graphite on Gampi Surface paper, 38 × 25 inches

Fallen from Grace

Meredith Sabini

We hunt and gather
in mall and market
garage sale, dumpster

Urban hunters stalk
cameras, laptops,
smart phones

This wild instinct
fallen from grace
into scavenging and theft

Won't die out
I know that now.
For it's why

I pick mustard
and miner's lettuce
in abandoned lots

Save wings and tail feathers
of birds that fly
into picture windows

Covet pelts of deer
    skunk and squirrel
    roadkill left to rot

And why I eat figs
    from the tree
    behind Stan's Exxon.

Timothy W. Graveson, *Farm Book,* 2008, photography, altered book

Poem

Judith Shaw

In the neighborhood lives a man by himself without a dog or cat or hamster, no cared for tree or bush or flower grows from his dirt, just discarded candy wrappers, cigarette butts, and toothpicks tangled in the dried clods of his landscape. When he walks by on his way somewhere the fresh blue air turns noisome sending a signal through the fences and gates on our street that he is passing.

Susan Putnam, *Untitled #216*, 2012, acrylic, ink, crayon, sand on gessoed silk, 12 × 9 inches

Shortcake for Breakfast

Ellen Shehadeh

THE DARK green, fifties-style house lay low and lanky. Inside, a musty shag carpet, gold-veined mirrored wall tiles, and a free-standing Danish fireplace spoke of Goodman's Lumber, 1973. A slimy, capsule-shaped shower resembled the orgasmatron in Woody Allen's *Sleeper*, without delivering, I discovered later, the corresponding pleasure. Elf-height pocket doors connected various add-ons: a large rumpus room and a small study.

It was not the classic country house I had been longing for.

It has more space than my tiny city apartment, I told myself. It's affordable, I told myself.

"It's not my dream house," I told the realtor.

"It's no one's dream house," he replied.

The pink and purple rhododendrons were in bloom. Ancient camellia bushes dotted the wild, untended garden. There was a redwood tree in a corner of the property. It has potential, I told myself. I might like living here full time one day. It has a rental cottage.

Anne opened the door to allow the potential buyer and her realtor to see the cottage. Lean, pale, and rumpled as if she had just woken up, she greeted me with a shy smile and fearful eyes, maybe wondering, Will she raise the rent? Will she ask me to move?

A small tabby cat scooted under the couch. Two large harps commandeered a good portion of the small living area, bookshelves overflowed, and the same Anita Brookner novel that was lying by my bedside also lay on her small table. I became aware of the stench of thousands of cigarettes—in the air, in the curtains, in the upholstery. The walls and windows were yellowed, the small refrigerator had a yellow cast. The once-white plastic shower stall was glazed with nicotine. I could see the concrete slab below the dirty, threadbare carpet.

I left quickly, feeling guilty and embarrassed, an undeservedly privileged intruder holding this woman's future in my checkbook. She didn't know that I, too, had been living in a small apartment for many years, was still a renter, and knew the jeopardy that all renters live with. I had no intention of asking her to leave or raising her rent. And being a private person myself, I would never again bother her at home, unless invited.

Five years passed. I was spending most of my time in my new home. With some major renovation, the main house gradually became more habitable. I rarely saw Anne. Although we lived within a hundred feet of each other, the cottage entrance opened onto an adjacent street. She always mailed her rent check and it was always on time. Once she came by to borrow something—I don't remember what. It was the only time she was ever in my house. She wore a 1960's miniskirt and platform boots. Her straggly hair hung below her shoulders. She mentioned that she had recently taken the train to Chicago, along with her harp, to have it repaired by the only expert she trusted.

One summer I noticed that her old beige Volvo was collecting leaves and looked as if it hadn't been moved in weeks. I phoned her to say that the utility company would be shutting off the water for a few hours. Her voice was very weak. "Is everything all right?" I asked. "Is there anything I can do?" She insisted everything was fine.

A few weeks later, on a Saturday morning, I sampled strawberry shortcake at the Farmers' Market and then headed to a local outdoor jazz concert with a friend visiting from the city. After oysters and white wine we drove back to my house. A sheriff's car and an ambulance were parked outside. Anne's sister had called the police after being unable to reach her by telephone. The police had found Anne dead in the cottage, lying by the front door, a half-smoked cigarette in her hand. Did I know anything about her? I knew nothing at all about my tenant. I had gathered she lived on a disability check.

The sheriff emphasized the probability of a natural death, but stipulated that only an autopsy could verify the cause. Feeling shocked and frightened, my friend and I fled to the city for the night, where we consumed a good deal of wine.

Very soon Anne's mother contacted me about coming out to retrieve her daughter's possessions, and in the course of our conversation I learned that Anne, who was 53, had been a champion ice skater in her youth, had attended prestigious private schools in San Francisco, and had been married and divorced. She had a developmentally disabled adult son, as well as a brother and another sister. Anne was scheduled to have all her teeth pulled the following week.

Her mother was warm, very proper, and grateful, I think, to talk with someone who had been acquainted with her daughter. It seemed the family was prosperous. They lived in an area of San Francisco with large, stately homes, and Anne's father was an attorney. Her parents had never visited the cottage and she had never given them her address. They had been sending the rent to her post office box, and her mother graciously offered to pay any rent past due, as well as for the following month while they moved her things.

I searched for the cat, but Anne may have run out of food both for the cat and herself some days before she died. Her cupboards were bare and the refrigerator empty. Just in case it was still around I left a bowl of cat food on the patio, only attracting skunks and a neighbor's cat.

Anne's family came to clear out her things. I stayed away, not wanting to intrude at such a difficult time. Knowing that a friend of mine was interested in buying the harps, I inquired, but her mother was definite about keeping them. Two weeks after the cottage had been emptied, I finally had the courage to enter, and then only accompanied by a good friend who was concerned about possible evil spirits, and insisted on burning sage in a purification ritual. I discovered some well-done pencil sketches in the storage shed, one a self-portrait.

Also left behind were a kitchen knife, a wilted African violet and a gold-veined tile. After many months and a complete gutting and remodel of the cottage, I began to feel that this dwelling actually belonged to me and not to the strange and sad woman who had lived there for fifteen years.

OVERLEAF Randall Gray Fleming,
Winter 1, 2013, digital photography

The Summer Palace Vase

Chris Reding

ON NOVEMBER 13, 2010 an Associated Press article flashed around the world: a stunning 18th-century vase from the Qianlong Dynasty that had disappeared from China under mysterious circumstances was rediscovered resting on the top of a rickety bookshelf in a bleak East London suburb. Auctioned for a record-breaking $83 million, the vase was bought by one of the rising class of young Chinese millionaires who sought to repatriate China's historical treasures. The tale of the Summer Palace Vase lingered in my mind's eye, tantalizing me with the story of the lives it might have touched.

When I was a girl
My name was Iparhan
And my grandfather was Khan Apak Khoja,
The ruler of the Uyghur oasis of Kashgar
In the prosperous wild lands of the Far West
Where the Silk Roads intersected.

While I was young,
All legs and lithe body,
Khulan and I galloped wildly across the steppes of the
high desert
Our horses reaching in long, flowing strides
Until in our squinted eyes the surrounding hills
Became a smear of red against the snow covered mountains.

The year Khulan and I married,
Emperor Qianlong and his Chinese battalions came
To conquer my people and seize our lands,
Raising great clouds of dust from the desert
And the sharp glint of blinding light
As the sun bounced off armor.

Unable to stand the waiting,
I rode toward the strange black clouds
That hovered over the fields,
And the great humming that filled the air.
The clouds scattered,
Revealing themselves to be hordes of flies
That masked the blood soaked land, covered
With the bodies of my people.

After the battle was lost and my husband, Khulan,
Dead in his father's arms,
Emperor Qianlong requested me
As his war prize.
And my grandfather,
Whom I had loved all my life,
Gave me to him.

The next morning both the Emperor
And I began our journey
To the Imperial Palace in Beijing.
Before entering the palanquin,
I was made to lie down,
To be swaddled in layers of felt.

Protesting,
I was told that it was the Emperor's order,
As a way to protect my body from bruising,
On the long and bumpy journey.
At that moment the precariousness of my position came to me.
I was no longer myself, but a Precious Object.

When I finally arrived at the Forbidden City,
I was carried in the palanquin with the Emperor's flag
Through huge red and gold gates to the Concubines' Palace
Past workers and guards prostrating themselves on the ground.
There I was greeted with shock and horror by the
        Queen Mother
Who saw me, a Uhygur,
As uncultured and a threat to all.

Within the Imperial Palace
Emperor Qianlong was also alone
Despite his absolute power.
With no friends or trusted confidants,
He was kind to me sensing
The loneliness and loss that engulfed me.

Since the outside world was now forbidden,
Qianlong built me a beautiful, walled garden.
As my heart softened towards him
I grew to be his friend and lover,
And was called Xiang Fei,
The Fragrant Concubine.

Seeking a deeper life,
I studied the history of China and the art of war,
And became the Emperor's trusted advisor.
Once, I suggested a strategy that won the day in battle,
And Qianlong sought to reward me with any gift I craved.
I asked to be Iparhan again for a day,
And to ride freely across the hills on horseback.

At the Summer Palace, where the Emperor could best
    protect me,
We rode out into the night light,
Qianlong tenderly savoring my joy
Knowing this moment could never be risked again.
The next morning when I woke,
I found a white silk-wrapped box fastened with a carved
    ivory branch.
Inside lay the Summer Palace Vase.

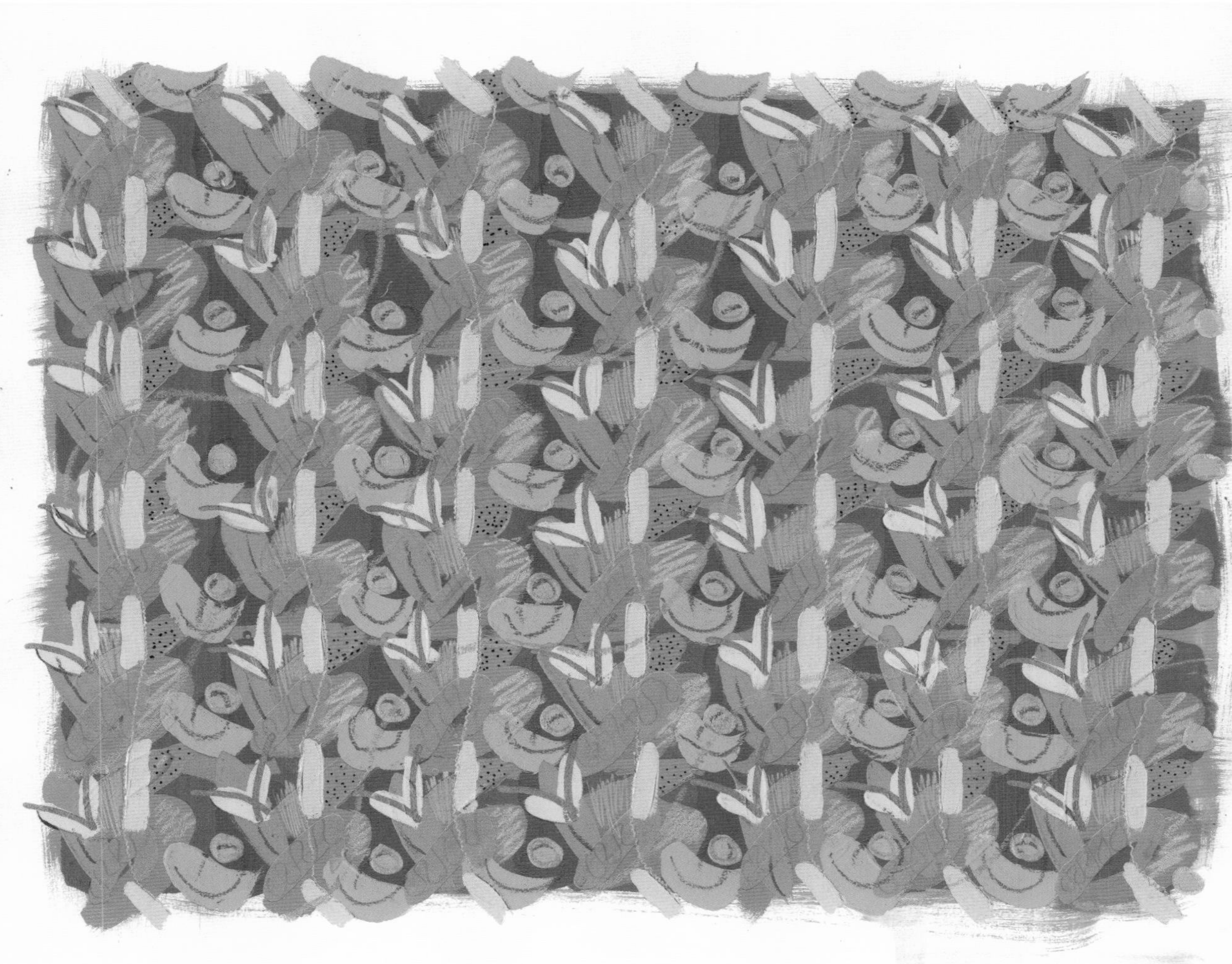

Elizabeth Hansen, *Green River,* 1992, mixed media on archival rag board, 24 × 28 inches

Morning Rounds

Muriel Murch

WHAT A GREAT sleep, nothing like a dying fire to turn throbbing pain into aches and twinges. I stayed on the small mat all night. I was not going to upset her by climbing into the chair. It's nice that she wakes up easily to let me out. I'll stick around a little this morning and see if she needs me. There's not much happening in the barn, Charlie Fox hasn't been over, just Millie and the other dumb young bitch from next door. Though I never see them, the cats must work a little because there aren't any mouse nests here. There, the horses are fed, and to thank me for helping she made me breakfast. That's a first for her, fantastic. Breakfast has been taken off the menu at our house. Now I'm ready to leave.

I go by the school, but the children are already in class and the kitchen door is closed. On through the eucalyptus grove. Three yearling deer with small velvet prongs are grazing in the dappled sunlight patch where they can eat and get dry after last night's rain. I give them the eye and we all acknowledge that this is not the day for a chase. I stop and drink at the stream. It's running fast and cools my feet. Two rats are busy housekeeping, preparing for a springtime family, but I'm not hungry and leave them for another time. Then it is on up the hill, through the marsh and across the open ground. It's O.K. if I stick to the road and travel alone. I only hear guns when I gallop with a friend through the cattle fields.

Here's my gate, the thick purple paint is glistening from the fresh rain. The house is silent, closed and cold. My bowl is empty and my mat is wet. There is no one home—again.

Notes on Inequality

Dean Rader

For Peter Norman, the third man on
the podium at the 1968 Olympics

It was his idea
to share
the gloves
and to be
in that moment
dangerously white.

The air
above him
was an open
hand waiting
for a baton,
hesitant, even
frozen, like
a neck
bent to receive
a medal.

Silver has
the highest
conductivity of
any metal. Its
name comes
from the Indo-
European word
for *shining*.

He never ran
in the Olympics
again. He was
shunned, hated
even, last in a
race that has
not finished.

What is courage
after all but the
absence of ego,
the dissolution
of the self in
the face of
annihilation?

Since the vertices
of a triangle
are assumed to be
non-collinear, it
is not possible
for the sum
of the length of two
sides to be equal
to the length
of the third side. It
is not possible
to be equal.

The third
wheel, the
tagalong, the
forgotten name,
the remembered
race, the lonely
moment during
the anthem
with nothing
but skin as the
accomplishment.

O to make
the nothing
everything, to
choose invisible
in a moment
of transparency,
to be the other
in reverse.

Debbie Patrick, *Are We There Yet?* 2012, pastel, 18 × 14 inches

Maxine

Joan Thornton

SHE WAS a deep metallic green 1951 Mercury convertible. In 1951 my husband and I, too young to be newlyweds, were struggling to pay the rent on a one-room attic apartment in which we had been arguing for a week about buying a new car. It was my opinion that we couldn't afford the monthly payments even with terms described as generous.

"Wait until you test drive her," my groom bribed.

"Have you forgotten I don't have a driver's license?" I asked.

In his prewar Ford we drove to the Lincoln Mercury showroom.

"You'll learn in no time. I'll teach you!"

I was not allowed to drive the Ford because in its old age it was sensitive to touch and would doubtless not survive the inexperience of mine. The elderly coupe stalled out at every stop, even under my husband's expert hands.

"RrrrGrr, RrrGrr."

"You're doing that on purpose," I said. I was forced to admit that we were always putting money into repairs that failed to end the Ford's persistent problems.

It was not the economic argument that lured me to the Lincoln Mercury showroom. It was the image of myself driving a car. I was still smarting from my failure to pass drivers' ed in my very recent senior high school year. I'd passed the written part of the exam, but I'd repeatedly demonstrated poor skill while parallel parking the school car. Even more discouraging had been my father's refusal to give me the extra driving lessons I'd begged for.

"Not in my car you don't."

My father had reason for his caution. Through a reward-punishment system in vogue when I was in kindergarten and first grade I'd learned, not without drama, to favor my right hand, but it often took me longer than most people to understand directions that included left-right commands. Despite that minor annoyance, I reasoned if could learn to write, surely I could learn to drive a car.

Every two years my husband's father bought a new Lincoln from Frank Worthington at Springfield Lincoln Mercury. It was only natural that Mr. Worthington should come forward to welcome us into the world of adult decision making. He beamed as my husband introduced me, saying how proud he was to be taking care of a second generation of car owners. Mr. Worthington, like my father-in-law, was a thirty-second-degree Mason, therefore reliable. When he mentioned a monthly finance figure, I asked, "What will happen if we can't come up with that amount every month?" He assured us he knew we were trustworthy and he would be there to take care of any problems no matter what. I wasn't sold. Not yet.

My husband was working on commission as a wedding photographer and I was employed as a film editor. Between us we earned so little we could rarely afford an evening out, and our slope-ceiling apartment was stuffy and hot in the late August heat.

From the air-conditioned dealership we stepped outside into the scorching show yard.

"Think about the wind in your hair," my husband teased, as I wiped perspiration from my face. I felt stubbornly responsible in my resistance, but I had yet to meet Maxine.

My husband and Mr. Worthington were talking about "she" and "her." She had or could get maximum everything. Maximum power, maximum mileage, maximum seating capacity, maximum torque, whatever torque was.

I no longer listened to the men as we stood admiring Maxine where she was parked waiting to take us on our test drive. I had to admit that her white walls were classy, her paint job sheer artistry, what with the maximum number of coats sprayed all over her long body by craftsmen imported from Germany. A subtle metallic frost glinted off a green so dark it was almost black. At the touch of a button on the dash, the cream-colored top slid smoothly, seductively, overhead, then relaxed into the well in back. It was like watching a scene in a film where a glamorous woman sheds a silver fox wrap and with nonchalant sensuality lets it drop out of sight.

The open convertible revealed honey-colored leather upholstery, baby soft to the touch.

"You just slide your little self along that seat," Mr. Worthington said as he opened the door for me on the passenger side. My husband was already seated at the wheel, looking as handsome and successful as a man in an Esquire ad. I knew by the expression on his face he would have sold our landlord's furniture and all of our wedding presents to own that car. Picturing myself wearing a dashing little hat with a long piece of chiffon floating behind me, kid gloves to my elbows, my graceful hands on the beige steering wheel, I, too, was ready to sign away my salary to own the car we were already calling Maxine for all her maximum endowments.

She was our darling and we took to driving around town even when we had no place to go. He wanted to go for a ride and I wanted to go for a driving lesson, but by the middle of September, I was more sunburned passenger than driver. We sat in parks and driveways as I tried to memorize the sequence of the gears and the H shape of the slots that the shift slipped into so smoothly for my husband.

"No, no! You are in reverse!" he said, clamping his forehead in theatrical exasperation. It was difficult trying to learn to shift from the passenger side, but we couldn't take a chance on me; I might strip Maxine's gears. I was always getting the clutch and the brake confused. My husband insisted I could not graduate to the driver's side until I got it right from the passenger's side. This was a far remove from the picture of myself as a confident woman of the fifties sailing down the Pike in her convertible.

"If you would only allow me to actually drive her," I begged. "We could start out on a country road."

His look told me I couldn't be serious.

As the New England summer was settling into a chilly fall, Maxine's top went up. Although she had a heater under the dash, Maxine wasn't as warm as a sedan, and when we went for a lesson I wore woolen gloves and a wool bandana that never floated out behind. Still on the passenger side, I continued to appreciate Maxine's purring engine and soft upholstery, even though two months after her purchase I despaired of ever being able to drive her.

Soon after the first snowstorm my husband lost his job. The studio he worked for went out of business and he found photographic employment with a detective agency. He was hired to take photos of married people in hotel rooms with people other than their spouses for the purpose of obtaining grounds for a divorce. The sleazy and infrequent jobs did nothing to improve his self-image. It didn't help that now I was earning the larger salary. Despite his irritated state, I persisted in my effort to learn to drive, only to fail again and again when we went out for my lessons. All we talked about was money. Inevitably, we had to choose: give up our apartment and move in with his parents, or give up Maxine.

We moved into the bedroom that had been his as a boy, and Maxine was parked next to my father-in-law's black Lincoln. I now needed two bus transfers to get to my job and I felt further away than ever from fulfilling my ambition to drive a car.

"The streets are icy. I'm not giving any driving lessons today. Just memorize the questions and answers in the driver's handbook."

"I know them by heart, inside out and backward," I snapped.

"Dear, he's right. It wouldn't be safe for you to practice in this weather." I had a sweet mother-in-law, but at that moment I was furious with her. Dramatically, I ran upstairs and into what was still referred to as my husband's room, and I sulked. From the window I could look down and see Maxine parked at the curb. The sun was shining. The ice on the street had melted. Maxine looked up at me and called in an Eartha Kitt voice, "Come on, I'll let you drive. We could have some fun."

It was early on a Sunday afternoon. My husband and his father were watching a football game on television. Taking the car keys from the dresser, I got into my winter coat and quietly slipped out the front door.

"I didn't know you could talk," I whispered to Maxine as I settled into the driver's seat. Feeling adult at last, I put the key into the ignition. Slowly, I let out the clutch and pulled away from the curb in first gear.

"I knew you could do that," Maxine replied, as halfway up the block she and I together shifted smoothly into second. A neighbor waved at me as if what she was seeing was perfectly natural.

I took a clean right on Dartmouth. I wanted to put the top down and call out to people on the sidewalk.

State Street was major traffic, six lanes of cars, buses, and trucks. Maxine and I started to feel nervous, but I decided we would be all right if I kept to the right-hand lane where I could pull to the curb if necessary. I was thinking about the position of the hand signal I would use to turn a corner. Straight up for right, stiffly out for left.

Suddenly, a city bus pulled tight beside me, looming larger than I thought it should. The bus driver was bending over in my direction, waving his arm as if he wanted me to do something. Speed up? Slow down?

"Oh no, now what, Max?"

She must have been as frightened as I was because she didn't say a word. Ah, there at the corner of the next block I spotted a big empty space at the curb. Trying to appear confident, I stuck my arm straight out. Why was the bus driver still honking at me? What was the matter with him? I turned the steering wheel to the right.

"It's O.K., Maxine," I assured the car. But it was not O.K. Trying to shift, I inadvertently put her into reverse and smacked right into the bus, which for some inexplicable reason had pulled in behind me.

It was there at the Lansing Avenue bus stop, me with no driver's license, slumping shame-faced at the wheel, the bus driver and a policeman outside talking, that my husband and my father-in-law showed up in the black Lincoln.

Maxine's rear bumper was crumpled and her brake lights were smashed. The bus was unscathed. The only thing my husband said to me when he opened the door was, "Move over." Poor Maxine, as shaken as I was, said not a word.

After returning a repaired Maxine to Springfield Lincoln Mercury, we moved to New York City, where we didn't need a car, and four years later, when we drove West, I was too preoccupied with a baby and a small child to take up the challenge to drive once more. It wasn't until the early sixties that I finally got my driver's license.

Last year, when I was driving through town, I passed one of those classic motor car clubs, a long line of perfectly maintained automobiles from the fifties motoring down the highway: a pink

Buick, a lime Oldsmobile, a maroon Studebaker, and yes, a green Mercury convertible. Her metallic finish was gleaming, her cream top was down, the caramel leather on full view. She called out to me in my Japanese car, her voice still deep and throaty. "I knew you could do it," I heard her purr.

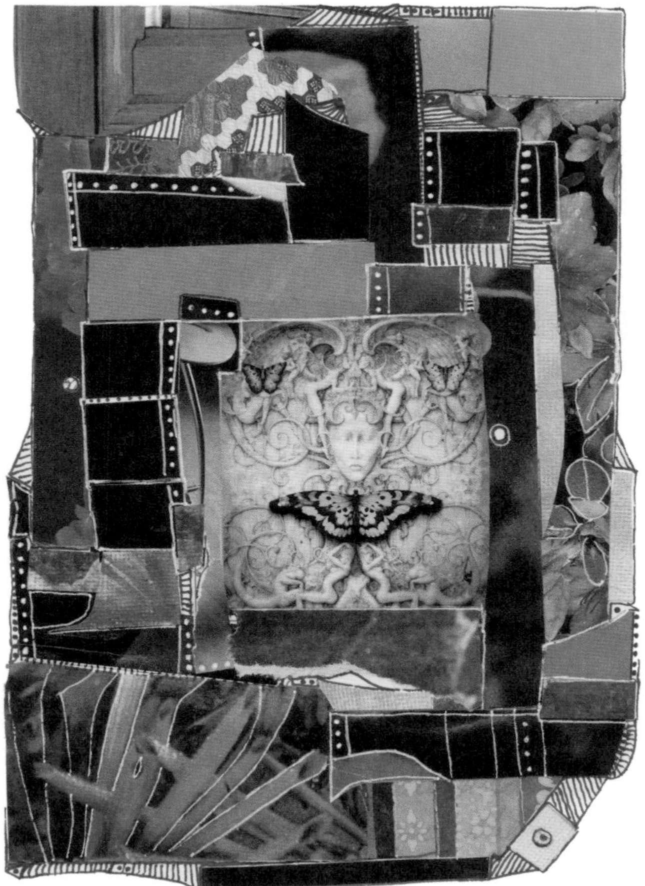

Rebecca Young Winslow, *Butterfly Collage*, 2012, paper collage, 5 × 7 inches

Nudibranchs

Celeste Woo

(Top) *Doto amyra*, 2013, silk, wool, cotton thread, 7 × 2½ × 1½ inches;
(center) *Flabellina iodinea*, 2013, wool, cotton thread, 7½ × 2½ × 1½ inches;
(bottom) *Triopha catalinae*, 2012, wool, glass beads, 5½ × 2 × 1½ inches

The Sand Swimmer

Claire Peaslee

DRAKES BEACH, early June, clear skies, midday warmth. Blond cliff in back, bay sparkle in front, variations on the color blue. Soon the sun's brilliance is playing optical tricks. The saturated sand, caressed by the waves' retreat, appears—impossibly—to rise and to churn, seething with totally un-sand-like action. Closer up—aha! A bumper crop of very new mole crabs is swarming through the sand behind a dropping tide. The dense mass of tiny individuals evidently "swims" downslope within the flowing substrate. Each time a wavelet soaks the shoreline, the entire throng seems to shrug a few inches seaward, and the sand's surface bubbles and heaves with their collective paddling.

This is indeed a spectacle of the littoral—that dancing boundary between sea and land. Yet this particular decapod, the ever-so-common sand crab, embodies the uncommon. While there are many ways for shoreline invertebrates to thrive in the presence of tidal rhythms, usually the main trick is to stick to one place fairly permanently, because just to be there is to be fed. The ocean delivers a continuous, dilute purée of organic matter, alive and dead, that intertidal organisms suck and filter with an astonishing range of anatomical devices. To succeed means essentially to stay put in the presence of crashing surf and churning tides—glue yourself to rock, jam your body into a crevice, burrow into sand or mud and live in a hole, or attach to someone else that has a holdfast or a muscle-foot or some glue-threads.

But what if your substrate is nothing like permanent, fixed, reliable, or even as constant as the muddy bottom of a bay?

What if you—and a handful of other not-very-mobile species—have figured out ways to plunder the ocean's nourishing soup kitchen on a pliable sandy shore where waves wash up and down? Sand dollars do this, as do certain bivalves (clam-like beings), plus a few of this planet's myriad segmented worms (that look like miniature monsters). But most of these creatures swim or wriggle or pump their way downward in sand, beneath the reach of wave action, and live far enough from the ocean's edge to be considered subtidal.

Just one among them prefers the meeting place of churning water and loose sand, a zone whose upper boundary is the curvy line on the beach where the waves halt their landward rush and change direction to flow back into the sea. Geomorphologists have given this sand-beach feature a perfect name: they call it the swash zone. All manner of physics formulae describe the forces at work in the swash: they deal in slope and curve of beach, interval and size of arriving swells, profile of offshore bottom, and direction and velocity of alongshore currents. All these things change, constantly and sometimes radically. There is tumult in the mix of sand and sea water known as swash.

Who loves the swash? Who travels hundreds of miles adrift at sea as a tiny larva, undergoing strange metamorphoses? Who ultimately body-surfs ashore along a sheltered beach such as that fringing Drakes Bay? Who seeks to settle out in a most unsettled environment—the swash?

The mole crab, that's who: *Emerita analoga,* sometimes called the sand crab. A cool little digger and swimmer in the maelstrom, a dweller in habitat that never stops moving and morphing. One of the more dynamic intertidal invertebrates you are ever likely to meet.

And yet so humble and seemingly helpless when dug from its comfort zone by a fisherman seeking bait or a child seeking close encounter with another Earthling. Only the size of a large grape or average kumquat, *Emerita* is drab-colored and rather indistinct, until close inspection reveals its finer attributes. That smooth, egg-shaped carapace, dull taupe in hue, is perfectly designed for movement through the sand with minimal resistance. Underneath, an *Emerita* may be brooding a parcel of bright-orange eggs, held by the flap of her posterior—an exoskeletal tail of sorts—that tucks underneath her abdomen. From April to October she can mate repeatedly and bear several packs of offspring, each numbering many hundreds or a few thousand, into the surf to float away—as far as Oregon in some years. The random-chance survivors will mature to grape-seed size and colonize another shore, another swash.

To enter in your mind's eye the mole-crab world, dig one very carefully from the saturated sand. Hold your captive gently between your thumb and forefinger, and watch its many appendages wave about in the air, seeking purchase in a more familiar surrounding. The hind legs are shaped like paddles, and *Emerita* may be actively using them to try to "row" away from your grasp. The real fun (for you and especially for the little crustacean) comes when you set it down on the wet sand, and in mere seconds it paddles right out of sight and downward into the swash again—backwards. *Emerita* is a back-stroke specialist, powered by the rowing action of its hindmost swimming legs, its pleopods. Its sudden hind-end-first merger with its substrate is endlessly impressive. I could watch mole crabs disappear into their sand-soup—backwards—over and over again for hours.

What I wish I could see, in a close-up cut-away view, is a mole crab foraging for bits of food. It positions itself vertically just below the sand's uppermost boundary and projects only the forward tip of itself up into the water. As the wave-wash passes overhead, *Emerita* treads water-sand with its back toward the land and belly toward the sea. The sea water then returns down the swash, and our hero unfurls a special pair of antennae, finely feathered and able to filter tiny diatoms and dinoflagellates from the dying surf. With a rapid rhythm—up to several times in the course of each wavelet's passage—the little crab draws its nets back in toward its face (let's say that crustaceans do have faces) and runs the goopy mesh through its multiple mouth parts, gulping down the bounty.

Meanwhile, the mole crab's second pair of antennae stick straight up into the water: they suck and squirt. Thus, *Emerita* is breathing. Ironically, this feeding-breathing activity also helps turn *Emerita* into food. Projecting tiny appendages creates little "V"s in the flowing water, which even you and I can sometimes spy if we watch the swash. Willets and godwits and especially sanderling know perfectly well what those little "V"s mean: lunch. Troupes of sanderling motoring up and down in the swash zone, rapidly probing in the loose sand and shallow water, are feasting on mole crabs, probably smallish ones.

And *Emeritinas* (fake word) do arrive teensy, having spent their larval lives as mere tidbits of biomass tossed about in the sea. When random chance favors their settling, they surf ashore, tumble out of the waves, and cling among grains of sand barely larger than themselves. Then they begin the habits of adult mole crab life a'swash: orienting relatively upright in the substrate, paddling while going with the flow—let's call it treading sand—suck-feeding, and growing large enough to reproduce.

By the time it reaches maturity, the female mole crab measures at most two inches long, the male just over half that. Adults may live another year or two, their purpose being to mate whenever conditions are favorable. One less-than-favorable condition might be crowding in the swash. Another, potentially offsetting the first, could be the occasional rogue wave that scoops up a dense bundle of *Emerita* and heaves it half a kilometer along the shore. Then, rising into this chaos, the multitude may paddle-surf like mad, riding the calamity together into a new, untested sector of the swash zone.

What a superb role model for resilience, for thriving through catastrophic change. Ah, *Emerita*, sand swimmer so fine, I stand in the swash and bow to your movement with (not through or against) upheaval—your timeless dance with impermanence.

Chelsea Buteux, Grade 12, Tomales High School, *Breach in the Pacific*, 2012, collage and acrylic on cardboard, 13 × 18 inches

Day After Easter

Helen Wickes

Leaden sky, as it's called, bearing down,
mausoleum gray. Whatever was meant to be,
was, and if meant to rise, did that, too,

without or despite us. In the shops they're selling
turquoise eggs. I remember my mother
year after year at dawn, stooping to hide

her hand-dyed eggs, blue and green,
in plain sight. On her face such pleasure.
I think of Jay DeFeo painting

her radiant starburst rose for years,
thousands of pounds of paint, the paint,
in some places, nine inches thick,

poised as she was for years between the seen,
dripping from her paintbrush,
and the unseen she painted toward,

in brilliant, white-gray bursting off the canvas,
out of the window, crossing the bay,
and merging with original light.

Atlas, running to fetch one apple,
the whole firmament briefly lifted from his back,
learned the meaning of weight
from one taste of lightness,
which is fragrant, a walled garden, whose trees
blossom and fruit.

What this has to do with Easter
is that a dark, thick, cold day draws a line
at your feet.

Dares you to back off, dares you smudge it.

Snapshots

Carla Steinberg

STILL LIVING in a twenty-four-foot Airstream, formerly silver, then puce, then a terrible pale green, I was one of the Queens of the Cove, so dubbed by the fisher and envelope painter who was fond of us all, though none rowed home with him at night. Back at the forge, the silversmith, his fierce mate, would have made sushi of any of us without a qualm. But it is not of the fisherman, hands splotched with paint, that I speak. It is about the man with a red TR3, he who played Caesar to my Cleopatra the year we read Shakespeare with a concert pianist as venerable as a great oak, who bore her own decline with Zenish grace as if The End were merely a glide over water. She adored *The Tempest* because the young sailors took part, making sheet-metal thunder for the storm. She read the servants' parts.

One late autumn evening, the full moon gleaming on the bay, the TR3 pulled up to my *palazzito* at water's edge in the rush of lapping tides. I had been captive there for five long years, stalled in mid-career after I left my formerly beloved, though between that then and this now I embarked on a thirty-six-foot cutter with one of the young sailors and his father, each a would-be captain of the ship and my heart. After four futile attempts to cross the bar to the ocean, which occasioned four more going away bashes, we slid through the mouth of the bay.

Mary Siedman, *Arroyo Hondo*, 2013, oil on canvas, 40 × 30 inches

I admit I jumped ship once they revealed we were en route to a little boat-to-boat contraband transfer in the tropical waters of the Pacific, and hence I visited hither and yon with two Mexican school teachers the length and breadth of Mexico, climbing this and that pyramid, boarding a jalopy bus crammed with people and poultry. They admired my Bohemian garb and long hair. I admired their ability to speak fluent Spanish, which I was endeavoring to learn by throwing the coins and consulting *La Biblia de China,* en Español. My *cabeza*, I confessed, was indeed *un melón*. Higher and higher we clambered, around switchbacks and hairpin turns, rocks scudding out from under the wheels, clankety-clank and over the edge. Finally, we arrived at our destination, a tiny pueblo as high as an aerie where we had come to visit one of the teachers' *abuelita* happily working masa on a stone.

Months later, on a small island off the coast of the Yucatan, I made enough fish tacos for thirty with *tienda* tortillas and barbequed barracuda caught, gutted, and grilled by my gringo pals while I snorkled along the shore, flicking my fins and gaping at the gorgeous hidden world through a clunky mask without benefit of corrective lenses.

After ranging through the mushroom fields of Palenque at daybreak and bathing in a shallow stream with the curious cows, after bagging the Ping-Pong tournament and writing the infamous *"El Viento de Frijoles,"* an homage to Mexican cookery, I returned to my beautiful bayfront property, i.e., the Airstream, for which, nearly a year earlier, I had forked over four hundred smackers, camping beside it in a Marin Surplus tent replete with Persian carpet and philodendron climbing up the center pole, before the sellers decamped. In this opulent if tiny haven, I feasted on cheese, avocados, carrots, apple juice, peanut butter, and Orowheat. There may have been brownies.

The driver of the TR3, a would-be barrister, so eligible, so appealing, so elusive, dressed in T-shirt and chinos, knocked on and opened the door, putting it to me: Would I care to drive to Point Reyes with him, and by the light of a gibbous moon filtering through bare boughs silhouetting the indigo wash of sky, paint the Station House—buff?

And indeed we did. Along with the rollers and the stiff-bristled brushes, he carried a big box of cassettes: Carole King, Aretha, Bobby Dylan, and the Fariñas. And in the morning after a night of rolling and rocking the house down, the walls shimmered a creamy pearl in the light of the warming sun.

Chelsea Buteux, Grade 12, Tomales High School, *Oncorhynchus kisutch (Coho)*, part of a series titled *Endangered Species of California*, 2012, acrylic on canvas board, 8 × 12 inches

Conversations with a Righteous Man

G. David Miller

I FIRST MET Meir Habermann when I was eighteen. He was a medieval scholar who had thrived poring over ancient texts at heavy oak tables in the university libraries of *Mitteleuropa*. I was a callow youth absorbed by rock and roll, the Boston Red Sox, and Elvis. It was 1960. My girlfriend and future wife, Susan, wanted me to meet her family in Jerusalem. And I was disappointed when I arrived in the dark, three-room apartment of Meir and Beila Habermann with its floor-to-ceiling book-lined walls and overstuffed armchairs draped with crocheted antimacassars. Susan's cousin was not a pioneer warrior out of Leon Uris, but a portly old man who shuffled when he walked, wearing Mason jar glasses at the end of his nose.

Abraham Meir Habermann was born in Zurawno, Galicia in the Ukraine in 1901. He was eighteen when he moved to Wurzburg to work for his uncle in the wine business, but he soon abandoned the business world to continue his studies at the university. At the age of twenty-one he took up residence in Zwickau, Germany, where he obtained a position as a teacher of medieval Hebrew poetry.

It was in Zwickau that Habermann met Salman Schocken, the founder of one of the first department stores in Europe. Schocken used his fortune to become an avid collector of ancient Hebrew books and manuscripts, and he invited young Habermann to catalog his growing collection. Meir divided his time between mornings at Schocken library and afternoons at the school where he taught. After a while, Schocken entrusted Meir with the funds to make valuable

Wendy Schwartz, *Conversation*, 2011, oil, 10 × 8 inches

acquisitions of rare books and manuscripts throughout Europe and the Ottoman Empire.

It was clear to Schocken very early in the 1930s which way the wind was blowing in Europe, so he moved his library to Jerusalem and asked Meir to be the full-time librarian. This invitation surely saved Meir's life. He remained in this post until 1967, during which time he became the foremost scholar of medieval Hebrew poetry, collecting for the library rare, ancient spiritual and secular Hebrew manuscripts. Meir was not only interested in the content of these texts, but he also wrote about their publication as craft. Among the hundreds of his own books and articles, he published monographs with such titles as *The Soncino Family as Printers* (1933) and *Hebrew Women as Printers, Typesetters and Supporters of Writers* (1933).

On subsequent visits I watched the way Meir handled a book. He caressed it, examining the type and the binding as well as the quality of paper. For him it was the greatest miracle that letters of any alphabet in infinite combinations could stream across pages of endless books on countless shelves of libraries, unlocking the mysteries of the world. I imagined Meir's wonderment equal to that of James Watson and Francis Crick as they decoded the molecules of DNA. It was, for Meir, no less than revelatory of the great power of the Almighty.

Words and their combinations consumed his life. Evenings, after supper, he tried to be helpful by wiping a dish or two. He would walk from the kitchen into the living room wiping and re-wiping the same dish while his mind worked out some anagram of greater meaning. He would pick a book off a shelf, revealing another row of books behind the first. He opened the book with one hand, forgetting the dish and towel in the other until from the kitchen, a reminder from Beila: "Neu, Meir, are you wiping?"

He might notice me sitting in a chair watching him. He would emerge from his reverie and acknowledge me with an enigmatic "Neu,

David, are you satisfied?" Then he went back for another dish to repeat the ritual.

It amused Meir to have me around. With a wink, he would call me a Lamod Vavnik, referring to an ancient myth that thirty-six righteous men hold up the world. (*Lamod vav* means thirty-six in Hebrew.) The story goes that no one actually knows who any of these Lamod Vavniks are except another Lamod Vavnik, the suggestion being that it takes one to know one.

On the Sabbath, I was never invited to the Habermanns' afternoon teas when local celebrities like the Nobel prize winner S.Y. Agnon or the great philosopher Martin Buber came to share a piece of cake. I was considered a slight embarrassment, unable to hold up my end of a discussion over some arcane bit of bibliography. But Meir was interested enough in me to take me to synagogue and reveal to me the beauty and sanctity of the words on the sheets of parchment of the Torah scrolls. These words were his dearest friends. He was so familiar with their ancient meanings that he was chosen to write the concordance of the recently discovered Dead Sea Scrolls.

∞

On Friday night, coming home from synagogue, while I tried to keep him from walking into oncoming traffic, Meir would stretch out his arms and say to no one in particular, "You can feel the peacefulness of the Sabbath descend upon this ancient city." One Friday, as we walked, he turned and focused on me. "I must tell you, David, of one of the gravest errors ever to befall humankind, that has had repercussions beyond measure." Meir and Beila had lost most of their family in the Holocaust, so I was prepared to hear him speak of that.

Instead, he started to quote from the book of Genesis: "In the beginning God created Heaven and Earth. He created light and he created darkness. He separated the land from the sea." Meir stopped and addressed me for the first time as a teacher regarding a worthy student. "What do you think the writers of this text were getting at?"

"I guess it was a way for primitive man to understand the world around him by creating a mythical power that brought order out of chaos." Was I repeating some chestnut out of my World Religion 101 course that I had barely squeaked through?

"Do you notice a theme here of recurrent use of opposition? 'Light and dark, heaven and earth, land and sea, order and chaos.' Do you know there is no word in ancient Hebrew for 'infinity'? How else to express the meaning of infinity except through the use of extreme opposites?

"Now later, in the Garden, there is this tree of knowledge, of 'good and bad.' Once again, the use of opposition. In ancient Hebrew, using these extreme opposites is the most felicitous way of saying 'tree of infinite knowledge.' By eating from this tree, humankind received the capacity to decode all the secrets of the universe, which, up to that moment, were the private domain of the Almighty."

Meir explained that stressing "bad" within this dichotomous phrase confounded the balance, poetry, and meaning of the original text. Later translations ultimately went further and replaced "bad" with the unintended notion of "sin." Sin was a Greek concept, unknown to ancient Hebrews. According to Meir, there is not even an ancient Hebrew word for sin.

This very religious man looked at me slyly and asked, "Why was the Almighty angry if there was no sin committed?" Not waiting for my answer, he said, "Neu, wouldn't you, too, be disturbed if your children had gained the power of infinite knowledge without possessing the wisdom to handle it? Knowledge without wisdom..." and he shook his head.

As we approached his apartment, Meir stopped and focused on me once again. "What I am trying to get at is that this simple story about man's exceptional access to unbridled knowledge is both celebratory and cautionary. And once it was translated into Greek and other languages, the meaning was lost. How has this become the judgment story of the fall of man rather than an exhortation to seek knowledge but use it wisely?" Meir shook his head in dismay. "Can you understand what trouble this has caused?"

I never again had such a conversation with Meir. Susan and I visited whenever we were in Jerusalem. Often, on Saturday, I would walk with Meir to the synagogue for the sunset service that ended the Sabbath. This was mainly to walk off one of Beila's heavy dinners. But there was also something special about being in Meir's presence, even when he appeared to be completely unaware of me. I recall standing next to him as he held the text in both hands, his lips moving in silent prayer, the only sound his lower digestive tract, like a ram's horn, steadfastly trumpeting praise to Beila's stuffed cabbage. Without ever looking up from his prayer book, he said, "Neu, David, are you satisfied?"

∞

In 1980, Meir died as he had lived—at his desk completing a volume on the Renaissance press of the Christian Venetian printer of Hebrew texts, Giovanni de Gara, with Beila sitting nearby as she had done over the past fifty years, proofreading his manuscript.

A few months after he passed away, I was in Jerusalem and went to the apartment to pay a condolence call. Beila was sitting in the living room that had received so many great scholars. She was wearing dark glasses in the dimly lit room. All the books had been removed from the shelves, donated to a new institute in Meir's name. I sat in one of the heavy chairs opposite her over a cup of tea she had just poured for me. She looked at me as if from a great distance and said, "Neu, David, fifty years? It's not enough."

Peace Process

Linda Pastan

The compulsive surge
of surf against rock, surf
against rock—
white shoulders of water
shattering to fragments,
reassembling
for another run.

The stubbornness
of rock—
unyielding shape of granite
cast off once
by a passing glacier—
arrogant now,
unmovable.

And over them both,
with its pastel ribbons,
the brief arc of a rainbow
(parent embracing two
warring children)
disappearing, color
by fading color.

Mark Ropers, *Limantour Scoters,* 2011, watercolor on paper, 16 × 12½ inches

Writers and Artists

BLAIZE ADLER-IVANBROOK, ninth-grader at Novato High School in the musical theater program of the Marin School of the Arts, loves photography, drawing, and singing, and plays electric bass guitar and ukulele. He also likes adventure.

BURT BACHARACH, singer, songwriter, composer, record producer, and pianist, is a six-time Grammy Award winner, three-time Academy Award winner, and most recently recipient of the Library of Congress Gershwin Prize.

Having moved fourteen times in her eighteen years, JASMINE BRAVO feels the need to capture once-in-a-lifetime moments with photography, so they will last a lifetime no matter where she is.

CHELSEA BUTEUX is eighteen years old and lives in Point Reyes Station. Influences from living in West Marin and Sonoma County have inspired many of her paintings.

FLORENCE CAPLOW is a botanist, Zen priest, essayist, and editor. Her books include *Wildbranch: An Anthology of Nature, Environmental, and Place-Based Writing* and *The Hidden Lamp: Stories from Twenty-five Centuries of Awakened Women.*

CELT CARR lives in Point Reyes Station, attends Tomales High School, and plays football as a lineman. He loves snowboarding and BMX free-style riding. He hopes to use his art to make video game characters some day.

Award-winning artist CLAUDIA CHAPLINE writes and paints in Stinson Beach. Her visual art and poetry have been published in numerous literary journals, anthologies, and books.

GINA CLOUD lives in southwest Sonoma County, where she writes, gardens, directs the Bloomfield Community Theater Group, and explores the hills and waters of Northern California.

RYAN CONNOLLY has grown up in West Marin and spent his life in the wilds of the Tomales Bay watershed. He attends West Marin School, loves to be outdoors, and especially loves to fish.

PETER COYOTE came from nowhere and is working his way back.

EMMELINE CRAIG lives in West Marin and paints with watercolors and oils to elicit joy and ease. She shows her work in her Blissful Gallery in Stinson Beach.

JUDY BRACKETT CROWE lives in Nevada City, California. Her stories and poems have appeared in *Prairie Schooner, Alaska Quarterly Review, Innisfree Poetry Journal, The Waterhouse Review, Squaw Valley Review,* and elsewhere.

ANNA DAL PINO is co-director of Mariposa Studio, San Francisco at Project Artaud. She and her partner, John, recently served as caretakers at Steep Ravine, Mt. Tamalpais State Park.

CLARE ELSAESSER is a painter living and working in Jenner, California with her artist husband, Kai Samuels-Davis. She daydreams daily of their future home in West Marin.

OLIVIA FISHER-SMITH is a sophomore at Marin Academy. She loves poetry, is a musician, and enjoys sailing on Tomales Bay.

RANDALL GRAY FLEMING's work has been exhibited at SF MOMA, Bolinas Museum, and elsewhere. Recent books include *Light at the Edge* (with artists Chris Reding and Jesse Fleming) and *Dottie's Harbor Cafe*. He lives in Point Reyes Station.

TIM FOLEY, a graduate of Harvard Law School, has represented death row prisoners and individuals accused of capital crimes for many years. His fiction and nonfiction have appeared in periodicals, including *All Hallows*, *Dark Hollow*, and *Wormwood*.

TIMOTHY W. GRAVESON is an Inverness native who works with books as subjects in conceptual photographic images.

JENNIFER GUTIERREZ is a Valley Ford resident attending Tomales High School, looking forward to college. She loves basketball and would like to be a crime scene investigator.

ELIZABETH HANSEN resides overlooking Tomales Bay and relishes her time spent as an artist and landscape architect in dialogue with the earthly and celestial realms.

GRADY SALAS HECHT is a fifth-grader at Tomales Elementary School. He is interested in making art, observing nature, reading, and sports. He lives in Valley Ford.

LYNN HOGGATT grew up wild in Berkeley, now writes, paints, and teaches in Paris, where she has lived for the past twenty-five years.

BRITTA KATHMEYER, MFA, is a German artist living in the San Francisco Bay Area. She is currently playing with matches, twigs, and other found materials to create drawings based on chance.

Since 1988, CAROLYN KRIEG has had forty-five solo or two-person shows. Her work is in museums and many collections. She's been awarded artist residencies in Newfoundland and Portugal.

BOB KUBIK has loved West Marin and its communities since he moved here in 1989. The people, in particular, fascinate him. Rick Lyttle was his etching mentor.

FRANCES LEFKOWITZ is the author of *To Have Not: A Memoir*, and has published numerous essays and short stories. She blogs about writing, leads writing workshops, and coaches/edits writers one-on-one.

Local librarian by day, undercover artist of different mediums by night, KERRY LIVINGSTON has lived in West Marin for many years with her husband, local historian Dewey Livingston, and her family.

CAROLYN LOSEE is a culture ecologist, published poet, and owner/principal of Archaeological Resources Technology in Tiburon, California. She serves on the Marin Poetry Center Board of Directors and coordinates the county's annual high school poetry contest.

CHANNON MILES, youngest of four, is a ninth-grade student at Tomales High School and a competition cheerleader for Pop Warner. She loves to dance and draw. She lives in Point Reyes Station.

Among forbearing friends and forgiving family, DAVID MILLER apportions his days between Marin and UC Davis in pursuit of answers to *why that's all there is; there isn't any more.*

ZEA MORVITZ lives in Inverness, has been drawing since childhood, currently uses graphite (mechanical pencil) or ballpoint pen on paper, and also makes artists' books.

MURIEL (AGGIE) MURCH is a nurse, writer, and farmer. Her published books, short stories, and poetry focus mostly on nursing and health. She also produces radio for KWMR.FM and PRX.org.

TERRY MURPHY is a builder and painter. His heroes include Wyeth, DeKooning, Diebenkorn, and Lincecum. He's currently painting a series on labor and the landscape, and another on the mechanics of baseball. He lives in Petaluma.

SARAH MYERS was born in England, then moved to Ohio, where she received her MFA in painting and drawing. She now resides with the coyotes in Olema, California.

HOWARD NORMAN lives in Vermont and has visited Inverness each year since 1969. His memoir, *I Hate to Leave this Beautiful Place,* was published in 2013. His new novel, *Next Life Might be Kinder,* will be published in May 2014.

LINDA PASTAN's thirteenth book, *Traveling Light,* was published in January 2011. She was Poet Laureate of Maryland from 1991 to 1995. In 2003 she won the Ruth Lilly Poetry Prize.

After thirty years of architectural rendering, DEBBIE PATRICK now pursues her first love, painting portraits and animals. She lives in Sausalito; her work has appeared in *Pastel Journal* and *Artists Magazine.*

CLAIRE PEASLEE, a naturalist and writer, investigates the ways humans experience the living world. Her life is informed by "improvisation of presence" (Action Theater), which she also sometimes performs.

EILEEN PUPPO is an artist, poet, actor, radio programmer, and board member of Gallery Route One in Point Reyes Station. She lives in Forest Knolls.

SUSAN PUTNAM of San Rafael approaches her drawings with the intent of looking beyond a fixed point in the work to allow the elements to unfold and remain fluid.

DEAN RADER's debut poetry collection, *Works & Days,* won the 2010 T. S. Eliot Prize. His *Landscape Portrait Figure Form* was published by Omnidawn in 2013.

CHRIS REDING is a Professor Emeritus of Fine Art. Her paintings have been shown in galleries and museums throughout California and, along with her photographs, have recently been included in the book *Light at the Edge.*

MARK ROPERS is a watercolorist and member of Point Reyes Station Open Studios. He is interested in presenting thoughtful, mood-evoking paintings of landscapes, water-related pleasures, and objects of interest.

MEREDITH SABINI, a fourth-generation Bay Area native, is a widely published essayist, award-winning poet, and author of *The Earth Has a Soul*. She is Director of The Dream Institute of Northern California.

STEVEN SATER, poet, playwright, lyricist, author, and screenwriter, has received two Tony Awards, a Grammy, the Olivier, and the New York and London Critics Circle Awards for his musical *Spring Awakening*, written with Duncan Sheik.

WENDY SCHWARTZ lives and paints along the marshlands of Tomales Bay. Whether agricultural landscapes or city interiors, buildings or figures, inspiration abounds.

JUDITH SHAW is a consulting psychotherapist. She is the author of two nonfiction books about the eating habits of Americans and is writing a collection of short stories.

ELLEN SHEHADEH has done radio interviews on KWMR and written for local newspapers since 1999. She has taught writing and is an avid hiker and loves animals, Bach, and gospel music. She has never had a cavity.

MARY SIEDMAN has lived on the Bolinas mesa for more than thirty years. As a painter, she concentrates on exposing the light and movement of her natural surroundings.

CARLA STEINBERG was born a nightingale, but due to the inclement Buffalo winters, tried being a blackberry bear before settling on the human form. Why? Pickled herring and a grandmother who sang to the chicken she was cooking.

MARGARET STAWOWY is a librarian and volunteers with a local poetry organization. A Chicago native, she currently resides in the San Francisco area.

CLAUDIA STEVENS works in watercolor and gouache with silverpoint and a dry-brush technique. She gathers plant specimens directly from the natural environment, sometimes hiking extensively.

Longtime West Mariner JOAN THORNTON writes, paints, constructs artists' books, and contributes to projects at Sometimes Books and Gallery Route One, both in Point Reyes Station.

SUSAN TROTT has published sixteen novels and many short stories, having devoted her life to the art of fiction. She also plays Ping-Pong.

BARBARA VOS educates herself by leaving hand and mind free to explore with paint. A child of 1950's Brooklyn, she now lives, paints, and practices Craniosacral Therapy bodywork in San Francisco.

HELEN WICKES's first book of poems, *In Search of Landscape*, was published by Sixteen Rivers Press. "Day After Easter" is from *The Moon Over Zabriskie,* which will be published by Glass Lyre Press.

There is nothing REBECCA YOUNG WINSLOW loves more than filling a page with something creative. She has exhibited in many venues, her favorite being the Petaluma Valley Hospital.

CELESTE WOO lives in Inverness Park, where she knits, felts, spins, and sews. She likes to look for nudibranchs at Duxbury Reef during the winter and summer solstices.

LAURA JULIET WOOD lives on a mountaintop with her husband and newborn daughter in San Miguel de Allende, Mexico. She is the author of *All Hands Lost,* published by Finishing Line Press in 2013.

West Marin Citizen
Speaking the language of West Marin
Citizen
Commission signs off on landfill plan
HOME DELIVERY!
Community Newspaper
Published Every Thursday
CATCH THE WEEKLY NEWS. Call 415.663.8232
Email editor@westmarincitizen.com Online at www.westmarincitizen.com

Your creativity is our business!

Joyce Kouffman
musician/composer/teacher
Joyce@JoyceJazz.com
415/663-9176

The Writer's Wilderness Experience

Lonner Holden, trail leader/writer

Come and adventure into the Inner Grand Canyon. In that timeless depth, connect with the heart of your writing where inspiration of light, sky, stone, river, and imagination pulse together at the source of creation.

EXCLUSIVE GUIDED RIM-TO-RIM BACKPACKING RETREAT

Contact: Lonner Holden (888) 840-3440
Email: writingwildadventures@gmail.com
(Limited to 6 participants.)

For itinerary, FAQ's, registration and current pricing:
www.writingwildgrandcanyon.com

west marin review

Volume 5

SPONSOR
Lucid Art Foundation

DONORS
Coastal Marin Fund
Jane L. Purington

IN-KIND DONORS
Cline Cellars
Preston Family Vineyards
Tierra Divina Vineyards
Tin Barn Vineyards

Thank you!!

About the *West Marin Review*

West Marin Review
Volume 5, 2014

ISBN 978-0-9822829-3-9

The *West Marin Review* is a publishing collaboration among Point Reyes Books and Steering Committee members Myn Adess, Mark Caballero, Madeleine Corson, Steve Costa, Doris Ober, and Ellen Serber.

Prose Reviewers
Nancy (Myn) Adess
Mark Caballero
Jim Kravets
Doris Ober
Ellen Serber
Kelly Thomas

Art Reviewers
Madeleine Corson
Sara Duskin
Mary Eubank
Thomas Heinser
Doreen Schmid

Poetry Reviewers
Donald Bacon
Willow Banks
Madeleine Corson
Robin Ekiss
Doreen Schmid

Volunteers
Calvin Algren
Bert Crews
Alvin Duskin
Sara Duskin
Jon Langdon
Amy Rainbow
Kelly Thomas

FRONT COVER Jasmine Bravo, Grade 12, Tomales High School, *Sister's Keychain*, 2013, digital photography

BACK COVER Terry Murphy, *Farrier*, 2012, oil on panel, 12 × 16 inches

Thanks to Kukuzo Productions, Inc. for permission to publish Mr. Sater's lyrics.

Managing Editor: Doris Ober
Associate Editor: Nancy (Myn) Adess
General Manager: Ellen Serber
Design: Madeleine Corson, Maxine Ressler, with Micah Johnson, Krista McCandless
Advertising Manager: Linda Petersen with Bonnie Guttman
Prepress Consultation: Jeff Raby
Bookkeeping: Meg Linden
Proofreading: Arline Mathieu, Claire Peaslee, Elisabeth Ptak
Distributor: Publishers Group West

SUBMISSIONS FOR VOLUME VI
Submission guidelines:
http://westmarinreview.org or
info@westmarinreview.org.

SUPPORT THE *WEST MARIN REVIEW*!
The *West Marin Review* is created through the volunteer efforts of friends, neighbors, artists, and writers. Donations are appreciated (and tax-deductible). You are invited to volunteer. To learn how you can help, write to info@westmarinreview.org.

West Marin Review
Post Office Box 1302
Point Reyes Station, California 94956